# Knitted Rag Rugs for the Craftsman

## 20th Anniversary Edition

## OTHER TITLES BY THE AUTHOR

Rugmaker's Handbook Series
*#1 Knitted Rag Rugs for the Craftsman*
*#2 Fabulous Rag Rugs from Simple Frames*
*#3 Crocheted and Fabric Tapestry Rugs*

Other titles:
*Traditional Shirred and Standing Wool Rugs*
*Bohemian Braid Rugs for the Beginner*
*Multi-strand Braids for Flat-Braided Rugs*
*Flat Wrap Rugs and Baskets*
*Introduction to Patched Rugs*
*Amish Knot Rugs*
*Broomstick Rugs*
*Chain Braid Rugs*
*Wagon Wheel Rugs*
*Anchored Loop Rugs (American Locker Hooking with Rags)*
*Bodkin Rugs*
*Introduction to Tambour Rugs*
*Knotted Shag Rugs*
*Pjonging and the Single Strand Chain Braids*
*"Hook Braided" Rugs; the Two-strand Attached Chain Braid*
*Kitchen Table Rugs*
*String Crochet Rugs*
*Primitive Rug Hooking, An Introduction*
*"Beaded" Rugs, A Unique Standing Wool Rug*
*A Rugmaker's Sampler*

Rugmaker's Handbook No. 1

# Knitted Rag Rugs for the Craftsman

## 20th Anniversary Edition
(revised)

*written and illustrated by*
*Master Rugmaker*

## Diana Blake Gray

*Rafter-four Designs*
Cocolalla, Idaho

# Rugmaker's Handbook No.2
# Knitted Rag Rugs for the Craftsman
20th Anniversary Edition (revised)



*Rafter-four Designs*

For infomation address:
Rafter-four Designs
P O Box 40
Cocolalla, ID 83813
http://www.rugmakershomestead.com

including information from:
*Knitted Rag Rugs for the Beginner*, Copyright 1985 by Diana Blake Gray
*Knitted Rag Rugs for the Craftsman*, Copyright 1988 by Diana Blake Gray
*Knitted Rag Rugs for the Craftsman*, Second Edition, Copyright 1996 by Diana Blake Gray



**ISBN: 1-931426-25-2**

Printed in the United States of America

**Dedication:**

To the members of my "advisory committee"
who have always been there.

# *Preface*

I will never understand why knitted 'rag' rugs have not been more widely made. They are easy to make (simpler and faster than crocheted or braided rugs) and quite durable. I really like the portability of knitted rugs, too. Most are made in sections that can be taken along for pick up work so you don't have to pack the entire rug around with you. The knitting is of the very simplest sort; the garter stitch can be used for all types of knitted rugs. Even if you are a beginning knitter, you will be able to make these rugs since only the most basic of knitting skills are needed.

Knitting with fabric strip has a unique feel that takes just a bit of getting used to. On the other hand, you get to make your own "yarn" from fabric. This adds a new creative element for even the most experienced knitter since each fabric looks and handles differently. Knitted rugs are not as heavy as crocheted or braided rugs, but they have a lot more body than the traditional woven rag rugs. Knitted rugs have a lovely springy texture underfoot and are easy to care for, making them ideal for use as accent rugs anywhere in the home.

It is likely that you already have the materials on hand to make knitted rag rugs and accessories. Old sheets, cast-off clothing, and even those fabrics that have been cluttering your sewing cupboard for years can be knitted into rugs.

In earlier editions of *Knitted Rag Rugs for the Craftsman*, I'd focused primarily on the creation of professional looking rugs for people who were particularly interested in going into the business of making rugs. This twentieth anniversary edition is greatly expanded with an eye to practicality. I'd found that many people were discouraged from rug making because of the time invested in preparing fabric strip. (With a professional quality rug, half of the time needed to make a rug is devoted just to cutting and folding fabric.) The simpler methods of fabric preparation in this edition will let knitted rugs fit more easily into a hectic lifestyle yet still be welcome additions to the home.

# *Acknowledgements*

No book about textiles can be said to be the product of a single person. Each of us has learned from uncounted generations of textile workers reaching far into prehistory. I have to acknowledge the contributions to this book of many anonymous men and women who left behind their rugs for me to find and try to decipher. I thank my grandmothers who passed down their textile skills and wisdom in doing even a simple job well. I also must thank the many readers who have written to me over the past 20 years with their questions and requests for information. They are responsible for many improvements in this edition.

Finally, I want to thank Peter Collingwood in England for showing me that being a textile structuralist is at least a *respectable* form of insanity.

# HOW TO USE THIS BOOK

This isn't a "craft book"—instead it is a handbook for the textile explorer. I'm not going to show you a picture of just one rug and say "Now here are the directions. Just remake the very same rug that I did." Instead, I'm going to show you how the various processes work so that you can take it from there to create your own rugs in your own designs. You don't need to be a textile expert or even an experienced knitted to use this book. All you need is a sense of curiosity and a willingness to explore new methods of turning leftover fabric into a unique rug.

While knitting has been used to make rugs in many ways, only a few techniques were ever documented and those sketchily at best. In this volume, all of those have been brought together in one place for the purpose of preserving the techniques by encouraging you to practice these skills. This book is designed as a teaching tool and reference handbook for those interested in learning to knit rag rugs. It is information dense with rug making instructions for many traditional methods that have never appeared in print, as well as new ways to knit rugs.

As an example, the chapter on how to knit a shaggy rug includes directions for five different techniques. One method was only cryptically described in the 1920's. Another is a method for which examples date to the late 1800's, but for which no directions were ever published. The other three are the products of my own experimentation designed to make rug construction easier, create a more durable structure and have reliable results for beginning rug makers using modern fabrics.

In 1985 I wrote the first book ever published exclusively about knitted rag rugs and, indeed, the first book to mention the basic methods in nearly 50 years. Each subsequent edition of this book has increased the previous number of methods covered as over the past two decades more old rugs have come to light and, of course, I've gained in experience and knowledge—especially in applying knitting techniques to modern fabrics.

I often hear from people who are astonished to find out that there are so many types of rag rugs. It is my hope that with this book, people will be astonished to find out that there are so many different ways to *knit* a rag rug.

**Part I** is a guide to the various knitted rug constructions, variations and techniques. These chapters are organized so that a beginning knitter can start at Chapter 1 and work up gradually to more complex and interesting rug structures. Or, if you are an experienced knitter, you can just pick a chapter at random and start in with the technique that interests you the most.

**Part II** is the "Handbook" section with all of the general reference subjects in a single place. It includes everything from selecting and preparing various fabrics for knitting to caring for your knitted rug. The directions for the processes that are basic to all of the rugs (such as how to double-fold fabric strip) and alternatives for stitch patterns are also in Part II. Different methods of casting on and casting off are covered as well as how to produce various edge finishes to show off your rug.

As you progress through the rug making chapters, you may find yourself wanting to use a different fabric than the example rug or enlarge it in size, or make it with a different stitch pattern or texture. That is when you'll find Part II very useful, and it is suggested that you look through the Handbook information just so that you know what is available there.

Due to the limitations of the printing process, the illustrations are more limited than I would have liked, but if you want to learn to knit rag rugs this is the book for you. Use this book as your guide to making knitted rugs and don't be afraid to try out different combinations as your own creativity suggests.

# TABLE OF CONTENTS

## PART II: KNITTED RUG HANDBOOK

# INTRODUCTION:

# *Knitted Rag Rugs in the Scheme of Things*

There are literally hundreds of ways to make rag rugs and knitted rag rugs represent only a small fraction of those techniques. Rag rugs of all varieties were virtually ignored by the textile establishment until recent years, being relegated to the disdained arena of "craft work" in contrast to "fine needlework." Knitted rugs were no exception. While knitting as a skill has been heavily documented in the past 200 years, the making of knitted rag rugs has not. Keep in mind also that excess fabric for making rugs simply wasn't available in most of North America until the middle decades of the 1800s. Only isolated examples of knitted rag rugs exist prior to the US Civil War.

Rag rugs as we think of them are a relatively recent development in textile history. It was in fact the Industrial Revolution that made it possible for rag rugs to develop at all. Before the invention of powered looms all fabrics, from the heaviest woolens to the finest linens, were hand-woven. Clothing and every sort of household textile were handmade and what little scrap was left was likely to be pieced into a larger item. Worn out cloth was used for cleaning, so there simply was not much fabric left to be used for rugs.

Water-powered looms began to replace home weaving about 300 years ago but it was the steam powered loom that really increased the speed of cloth production and lowered the cost of textiles by the mid-1800s. It is from approximately that time that many of the rag rug methods originate.

Some of the methods used for rug making were a simple substitution of fabric strip for yarn in older textile constructions. For example, knitting has roots reaching far back into history so it was a natural step to move from knitting with yarn to knitting with fabric strip. Particularly since knitting was a widespread household skill, it was a simple conversion for people to make and early references to knitted rugs are vague because it was presumed that everyone knew how to knit.

Other methods used for rag rugs followed this same progression. Some creative soul simply wondered if a familiar process would work with a different material. Examples of this type of transition include: crocheting, naalbinding and hooking which all substituted strip for yarn; and braiding, flat wrap, twining, etc., which substituted fabrics in older basket-making techniques for natural fibers such as straw, rushes, bark and grasses.

It is by no means however that all of the rag rug methods were simply a new application of an older textile process. Indeed, the most interesting of the rug making methods seem to have developed *because of* the availability of excess or waste fabric. Remember that having any fabric "left over" was an unfamiliar concept, so in many ways scrap fabric became a completely new material to be put to use. Prodded rugs are a good example of a technique that seems to have developed (in Britain) as an application for leftover fabric. It was not a technique that lent itself to the use of yarns, but instead made use of a resource that had not existed before.

Another factor in the development of such a broad range of methods appears to be the cross-cultural influences that occurred during the settlement of North America. Pioneers on the frontiers came from many different textile traditions which seem to have combined to create new techniques or variations in rug making. And of course, here and there an extraordinary person had a feel for working with fabrics in rugs, so some of the techniques seem to have sprung from just a single inventive person. This is indeed still going on today and so the progression of rug constructions should not be considered a closed subject.

In the middle and late 1800s knitted rag rugs were regarded as utilitarian and directions for their construction are minimal. The garter stitch was used. Color schemes for the dying of the rags were sometimes included.

*To Make Rag Rugs.*
*"Cut rags and sew hit and miss, or fancy striped as you choose; use wooden needles, round, smooth, and pointed at one end of any convenient length. The knitting is done back and forth (like old fashioned suspenders), always take off the first stitch."*
*(1885, "Buckeye Cookery")*

*Knitted and Crocheted Rugs*
*"If one has plenty of old delaines or thin woolen goods, she may tear them in strips a half inch wide and knit them on coarse wooden needles or crochet them with a large crochet needle, and arrange the different colors tastefully, sewing or crocheting the knit strips together, and surrounding the whole with a border of fringe or fancy-cut pieces. This kind of a rug keeps its shape better if lined with a firm piece of crash or bagging."*
***(1871, American Farm Journal)***

During the Arts and Crafts period (roughly 1890 to WWI), design and quality of construction was emphasized and wedge knitting is first described. Amy Mali Hicks wrote *The Craft of Handmade Rugs* in 1914, which became a standard reference for rugs and was reprinted many times until the late 1930s. Her writing influenced rug making through that period. Her book describes a strip construction rectangle (which she refers to as "oblong" in the following excerpt) and a circular wedge knit rug.

*Hick's Oblong Rug, 1914*

*"The knitted rug is another rug which has reached the satisfactory standard of modern craftsmanship and is also a striking example of how successfully a rug based on a humble craft can be made if well-planned. Surely to paraphrase a familiar quotation, "The plan's the thing." The craft of knitting cannot be said to possess any technical difficulties. Almost any one can knit, though to be sure even so simple a performance as this can be done more or less well. But anything that is easy finds inexperienced enthusiasts, so the knitted rug of the hit or miss variety is more frequently met with than one which is carefully planned.*

*"Before the present revival in the handicrafts the old Colonial looms on which the farmer folk did their own weaving were discarded as old-fashioned and cumbersome and so when rugs or carpets were needed and there was no carpet weaver conveniently enough located to weave up balls of cut rags, the knitting needles were resorted to and the knitted fabric took the place of the woven one. ...*

*"The materials generally used for making knitted rugs are old rags of either wool or cotton. This accounts to some extent for their somewhat uncared-for appearance as the design cannot be as well controlled...*

*"Since the materials from which these rugs are knitted, make a thick thread when cut into strips, the fabric itself is heavy and to make it easier to handle the square and oblong rugs are made in bands from eight inches to ten inches in width, and are afterward sewed together."*

***(Hicks, Amy M. The Craft of Hand-Made Rugs**, McBride, Nast & Co., NY, 1914)*

During the 1920s, contemporary publications embellished knitted rugs emphasizing their artistic points and sometimes specifying silk as the material of choice as in the following excerpt.

[illegible]

***Bowles' Fluff Mat, 1927***

*"Now let me tell you of a splendid way to use up bits of silks or knitting worsteds by making a 'scrappy' knitted rug. Long bone or wooden needles, a ball of heavy white knitting cotton, and a box of silk scraps about an inch and one half long and an inch wide—these are the required materials. Cast on thirty-six stitches and knit once across. On the next row, after knitting two stitches, knit a scrap of silk into the work. Knit two more plain stitches, then knit in another scrap of silk.*

*"Continue in this manner until the row is completed. Knit back across plain without any silk scraps; then knit another row, using two plain stitches and the third with silk scraps, until the rug is of the desired size. Five strips are needed, and usually the rug is square in shape. Hit-or-miss centres with deep black borders are pretty for these. After the strips are sewed together, the whole may be lined with heavy cotton cloth."*
*(Bowles, Ella S.,* ***Handmade Rugs****, Little, Brown and Co. 1927)*

As the twentieth century progressed, rag rugs experienced periods of popularity and decline. The Depression era of the 1930s was an economic incentive for home manufacture of rag rugs but more affluent periods seem to have relegated the practice to a quaint outdated pastime with overtones of poverty. During the Depression of the 1930s Hicks' book remained a standard and knitted rag rugs were fairly widely made. Quite a few examples of the wedge knit rag rugs have survived from that period. The rationing of the war years of the 1940s extended the practice of knitting with recycled clothing and stockings. Following World War II, references to knitted rugs became nearly the exclusive province of yarn and thread companies and the techniques of knitting with fabric strip gradually disappeared in favor of knitting with rug yarns. The prominence of knitting rugs with yarns continues to the current time, but interest in the revival of handwork of all sorts has brought knitted rag rugs increasing popularity.

These various influences, from ancient to modern times have created unlimited possibilities in rag rugs. The varieties of surface texture in knitted rugs alone range from the smooth and flat to rough and shaggy. Since so many different materials can be used with a single rug making method, it is possible to have the "same" rug look ultra-modern with a shiny high-tech finish or rustic and primitive. In short, knitted rag rugs belong almost anywhere these days and only the rug maker's imagination is the limit.

# PART I: KNITTING RAG RUGS

## CHAPTER 1

## *Starting Simply with T-Shirts*

In the finest tradition of rag rugs, this first project recycles an old T-shirt or two into a hotpad or the start of a rug. T-shirt knits are one of the easiest materials to prepare for knitting and the strip handles very similarly to yarn, so a beginning rug maker will face the fewest difficulties in getting started.

**You'll Need:**

- a pair of knitting needles size 15 (10 mm) at least 10 inches long;
- a pair of sharp sewing scissors
- a large-eye lacing needle or tapestry needle or a large safety pin; and
- a large man's T-shirt or two smaller ones.

Using the scissors, cut the bottom hem off the T-shirt and then cut around and around the T-shirt in a spiral creating a continuous strip about one inch wide. Stop cutting when you reach the first underarm sleeve seam as shown in the illustration. Usually the cutting process goes most quickly if you slip the T-shirt over the end of an ironing board and rotate it toward you with each cut. For a little extra strip, the sleeves can also be cut into a spiral if you wish. (Don't discard the top portion of the T-shirt, since it can be used in knitting a shaggy rug in Chapter 4.)

When the strip is cut, take a section about two feet long and stretch it out. You'll see that it curls into a neat little tube. Don't pull so hard that you hear any tearing or pop any seams, but the two foot section will stretch to a little over three feet in length. When all of the strip is stretched, roll it into a ball and you're ready to start knitting.

The small side seams of the T-shirt will curl to the outside of the strip when using the spiral cut, but don't be too concerned about them at this point. The seams aren't prominent. (If you look closely at the knitting shown in progress in the illustration, you'll be able to spot some of the seams.) Remember that this is a practice piece and there is information about how to handle knits so seams don't show in the Handbook section in Part II when you want a more finished look.

These directions are for an 8-inch square hotpad in the garter stitch, but the important part of this exercise is to demonstrate how nice knitted rugs feel underfoot. So play with the hotpad as if it were a mini-rug. Set it down on the floor, step on it, look at how the texture appears when viewed from a distance. People are invariably surprised at how appealing knitted rugs are. You may find that you like it so well that you want to grab another T-shirt and keep going.

**Directions for 8-inch square hotpad in garter stitch**
(There are other stitch patterns and shapes to try in the Handbook section, but for your first practice piece stick to the garter stitch while you get the feel of knitting with fabric strip.)

Cast on 18 stitches, leaving about 6 inches of strip at the beginning
Slip 1, Knit 17 (Repeat until 32 rows are completed or your hotpad is roughly square.)
Cast off

Pretty quickly you'll get the idea that working with fabric strip is a little different than knitting with yarns even though T-shirt knits are the easiest to handle. The trick to knitting with fabric is to keep your work relaxed, not tight, and to use just the tips of the needles in making the stitches. The first three rows of knitting will be the most awkward, so keep on until you begin to feel natural handling the strip.

*Remove the hem from a T-shirt, then cut strip one inch wide in a spiral ending at an underarm seam.*

*Gently stretch the strip to make it curl into a neat tube. Below is a cotton T-shirt strip before and after stretching.*

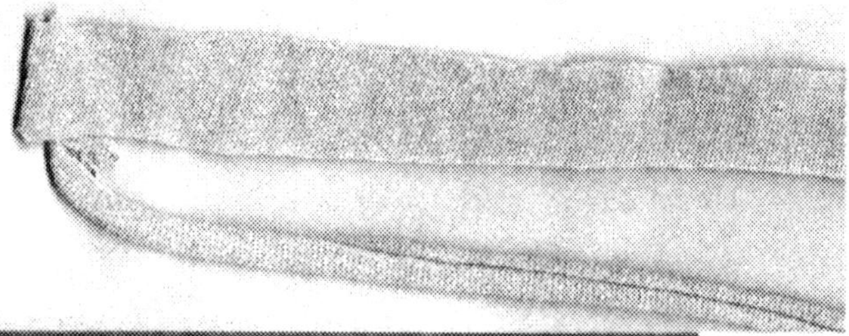

*Knit with the T-shirt strip just as if it were yarn.*

*Shown is a beginner project, a hotpad in the garter stitch.*

You may find that your knitting does not measure eight inches across. Knits, like all fabrics, come in different weights and get thinner with wear. If you used a well-worn T-shirt, your knitting will likely be narrower. If you used a more heavily made or newer T-shirt, the knitting may be more than eight inches wide. Don't worry about the width (or gauge), just note that it will vary with the weight of the materials used.

When you've cast off, clip the fabric strip about six inches from the last stitch. Then use a large-eye lacing needle, tapestry needle or even a large safety pin to work the tag ends of the fabric back into the knitting and it's all done. If you want to have a loop to hang the hotpad from, just sew a small loop in the strip before you lace the ends in.

Most households have a pretty good collection of unused and outgrown T-shirts, turtlenecks and similar lightweight single-knit clothing, so it can be a lot of fun just to keep going to make a rug (and clean out the closets at the same time). T-shirts with large, rubbery, printed areas may not cooperate very well since the printing stiffens the fabric and will generally keep it from curling up neatly.

T-shirt knitted rugs are an excellent choice for beginning to knit rugs and quite a few rug makers never bother with any other materials. If you do decide to keep going with your rug project, you will need to sew together the strip made from each T-shirt to make a continuous length. See the Handbook section for the "bias joint" for instructions on that process.

In the following chapters you'll see instructions for rugs of many different styles and shapes. Any of them can be made with T-shirt fabrics, so don't feel limited on choices. The only real drawback to T-shirt rugs is that they aren't as quite as durable as rugs knitted with woven cotton fabrics (like calico) so don't plan to use them in a heavy traffic area or as a scuff mat.

## CHAPTER 2:

# *Three Sheets to the Rug*

Traditionally rugs have been knitted from lightweight woven fabrics, usually cottons. These are a little less cooperative than T-shirt knits since they don't have any built-in stretch. It takes a little practice to get the feel of knitting with these materials, but once you acquire the habit of working just with the ends of the knitting needles the work goes quickly. You will find that every fabric has its own "natural" stitch size, which it wants to form. Don't fight with the fabric—it will win, and make more work for you. If you find you are struggling to knit a stitch, it means that you have been working too tightly and trying to force the fabric to a smaller size than is natural for it.

Having the right needles also makes a difference in how easily the knitting goes. The needles should have long tapered tips and a very slick finish. (See the Handbook section for a more extensive discussion of appropriate needles.)

The first projects using woven cottons will specify strips cut or torn to a one-inch width. Strips of this width are used unfolded and will knit more easily than the strips used for professional quality rugs (which are 1½ inches wide and double-folded). These unfolded strips do have a little more rustic appearance in the rug, but are prepared more quickly.

For this simple first rug, all that is needed are three twin-size flat sheets. These can be new or used. I will admit up front that that I went out and bought three sheets for this example rug. The twin sheets are the ones that always go on sale first and the price was $4.00 each for a total material cost of $12.00 for the rug. I always look for the ones that have a thread count of 200 or more, but any sheet with a 150 thread count will work. Avoid the muslin sheets with a thread count of 120 or 130 since they really don't have enough substance to hold up in a rug. Sheets are one of the best buys around for new fabric since a twin flat sheet has the equivalent amount of fabric of four yards of 45-inch wide cotton. (If you have sewing fabrics that you'd rather use for this rug, you'll need 12 yards total.) If you are using old sheets, hold them up to the light. If they show a thin spot in the middle, only use the side portions for rug making.

If you aren't confident of your rug-designing ability yet, use three sheets all of the same color. For a slightly bolder look, choose sheets of two or three coordinating colors.

## *How to Make the Overlapping Bias Joint*

*The overlapping bias joint is used to join unfolded strips from any woven fabric, regardless of weight or width of strip. The seam itself is sewn on the bias of the fabrics and spreads the bulk over sufficient distance that it isn't prominent in the finished rug. (For strips that will be double-folded and for knit fabrics that will curl, do not use this joining. Instead see the Handbook section for the regular bias joint.)*

*Lay the two strips to be joined with one on top of the other, overlapping the ends about one inch. If your fabric has a "right" side, make sure that the right sides of both strips face the same way.*

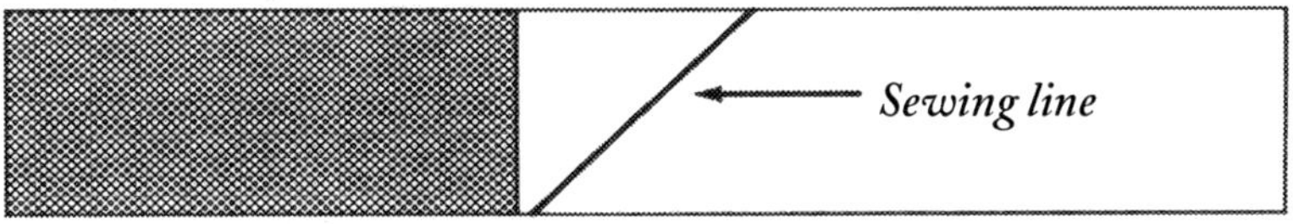


*Sew diagonally across the overlapped section to join the two strips.*

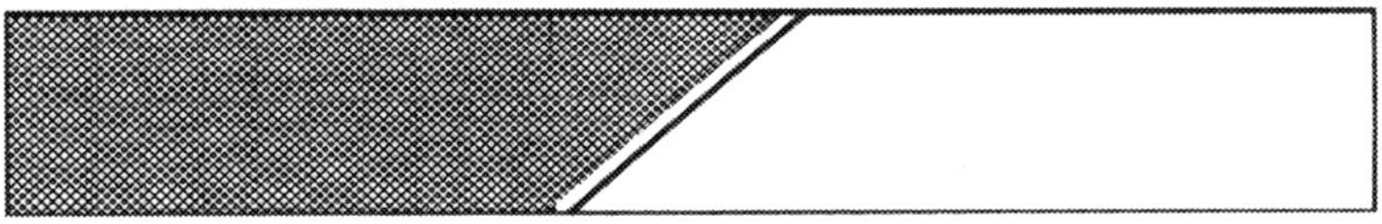

*Trim the corners, on both front and back, leaving about a 1/4-inch seam allowance.*

New sheets or fabrics should be pre-washed to remove any sizing and soften them. The fabrics can be either torn or cut to the one-inch width. Believe it or not, torn strips will actually result in a less thready rug when using unfolded strips. To convert your sheets (or fabric) to rug strip, cut off any hems and remove the selvages as well. The selvages can be torn off to give you a straight edge for tearing more strips. Clip along one edge at 1-inch intervals and tear down the length of the fabric or sheet.

Be sure to remove the loose threads from the strip with each tear or an unholy tangle will result. Sew the strips together to form a continuous length using the "overlapping bias joint" shown in the illustration. Roll the strip into a ball.

This rug is made in three sections, which can each be a different color made from a single sheet. For that look, sew all of the torn strips from one sheet together and roll it into a separate ball. If you'd like to try a more interesting look, the fabric strips from the three sheets are mixed up together to create stipes of color in the knitted rug. The strips from each sheet are sewn in the following order. For the sake of clarity, I'll refer to the three sheets as light, medium and dark.

Light fabric: 2 strip
Medium fabric: 4 strips
Dark fabric: 2 strip
Light fabric: 4 strips
Medium fabric: 2 strip
Dark fabric: 4 strips

The sewing sequence then repeats from the beginning with two strips of the light fabric. Roll the strips into balls as they are sewn together. When a ball of strip is a little larger than a softball, complete the next sequence of sewing and then start a new ball. That way each ball of strip begins and ends with the same fabrics. When all of the strips are sewn and rolled up, you're ready to start knitting.

The directions below are for the garter stitch, but if you've made a small practice hot pad, and are ready for a little more interesting texture, you can use the shingle pattern stitch. See the section on alternate stitch patterns in the Handbook in Part II.

**Knitting the Rug:** Use size 15 (10 mm) knitting needles 14 inches long, or circular
Cast on 22 stitches, leaving about 6 inches of strip at the beginning
Slip 1, Knit 21

Repeat until 96 rows are complete for a strip three feet long.

Don't use up all of the strip since you will need some for lacing the rug together. Cast off all of the stitches and pull up the end of the remaining strip through the last stitch. Pull up 5 or 6 *feet* of strip through the last stitch to use for lacing the rug sections together. Repeat the knitting procedure for the other two knitted sections, completing the same number of rows as the first.

Arrange the knitted strips side-by-side, turning them and rearranging them until you like the look of your rug. Then take adjacent knitted sections, thread the end of one of the long pieces of fabric strip through the eye of a large-eye lacing needle or tapestry needle and you are ready to start lacing the rug together. Work on a table or any flat surface for the lacing. I really don't recommend the floor for this process if you have pets or small children around. Handmade rugs are magnets for kids and dogs and cats and if you lay the rug on the floor, they will be on top of it in short order.

The easiest lacing procedure is to use a whip stitch—going down through one row and up on the matching row of the other knitted section. Do this twice at the very first and very last row of the knitting to make sure of the edges. Lace every pair of rows together. Don't skip any or you'll have a hole in the rug and have to go back with some more fabric strip to fix it.

When you have the two sections laced together, lay them down on the floor and make sure that the lacing isn't so tight that they bunch up. Lacing should hold the sections firmly together but still be loose enough that the knitted sections lay easily side-by-side. If you do have some sections that look too loose or too tight work back up the lacing to adjust the tension.

Once the lacing is right, use the lacing needle to weave the end back into the knitted section and hand-sew it in place. Clip off any excess. The hand-sewing keeps that end from working loose when washing the rug. Do the same thing with the tag end of fabric strip that was left when you cast on the stitches.

If you want to "frame" your rug, look through the Handbook in Part II for the various edgings that can be used with knitted rugs. Edging isn't usually necessary with rugs made in the garter stitch, but if your rug is going to be used in a high-traffic area, the edging will protect the rug itself from wear at the edges.

*Knitting a rug from torn sheets, alternating colors to form horizontal stripes.*

*After the strips are knitted, they are laced together using fabric strip and a lacing needle. Shown is an expanded whip stitch lacing. Note that in actual lacing, the stitches are pulled tight.*

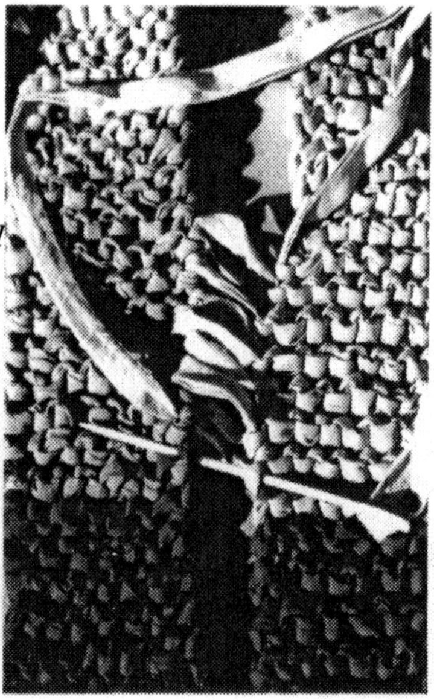

*The completed rug from three sheets. The colors run across the rug generally and the appearance is rustic.*

## CHAPTER 3

# *Knitted "Strip" and "Block" Rugs*

Strip and block style knitted rugs are the simplest to construct and so are probably the two earliest types of constructions. The terminology can get a little confusing though, so first a bit of explanation. With "strip" rugs, the knitting is done in fairly narrow sections that are all the same length—just like in Chapter 2 where each strip is knitted with a sheet—and then joined together side-by-side. By changing colors frequently in a strip of knitting, different blocks of color will appear, but the rug is still a "strip" rug.

In a "block" rug, the knitted sections can be any shape such as hexagonal, square, rectangular or even long knitted strips, but they are oriented in different directions. The "log cabin" pattern later in this chapter uses mostly long knitted strips, but they are oriented around the rug in various directions, which makes the log cabin pattern a "block" type rug.

Another distinction in how "strip" and "block" rugs are made is in the knitting itself. Knitted "strip" rugs can be (and should be) made with a specific number of rows in each knitted strip so that they can be laced together matching row to row on each side. Several sections can be knitted and then all laced together at the same time. "Block" rugs on the other hand are made of sections that are knit-to-fit a previous section. With block rugs, the row count is disregarded entirely, and each section is laced to the rug as it is completed. Because of this limitation, people often look upon block rugs as more complicated to make, but in practice they are actually simpler since you don't have to worry about gauge or counting rows.

For both strip and block rugs, it is important to make sure that you have enough of each fabric so that you don't run short before your design is completed. See the Handbook in Part II for how to graph your design to determine the fabric requirements for a rug.

Strip and Block rugs also offer the most options for alternative stitch patterns. Since neither strips or blocks need to bend around curves, the more rigid and structural types of knitting stitches can be used in these rugs. In the Handbook section of Part II are several alternate stitch patterns that can be used with any of the rugs in this chapter. The directions for these projects are in the basic garter stitch, but don't feel constrained by that—just substitute the alternate stitch pattern when following the basic directions.

**Simple designs in "strip" rugs.**

Strip knitted rugs can be made in a wide variety of designs. The traditional pattern is to combine fabrics at random as you knit, then join the strips together. This is the "hit-or-miss" design and can be quite attractive, but for a more finished or contemporary look, you should plan for the placement of the rows of each color in the knitting. On the following pages are simple variations of a basic knitted strip rug using just two or three colors.

**Simple Designs for Knitted "Block" Rugs**

Square or rectangular blocks of knitting can be assembled with each block of knitting laying in a different direction around the center. Each block is laced to the rug itself as soon as it is knitted to make sure of an exact fit. You can also use the idea of blocks to form a border for a strip knitted rug.

**The Classic Log Cabin.** One of the easiest of the block rugs is the knitted "Log Cabin"—so called because it resembles the quilt pattern. A center square is knitted and then bordered with sections of knitting going around the center in sequence. Every block can be of a different color or the quilt pattern can be imitated by two sections of the same color being set together at the corners.

The center square can be of any size and the best proportions are preserved if the blocks bordering it are made about half the width of the center square. For example, if you have knit a center square 28 stitches wide, the bands of color bordering it should be knitted 14 stitches wide. For a very large center square, use circular needles or piece together two narrower sections of knitting.

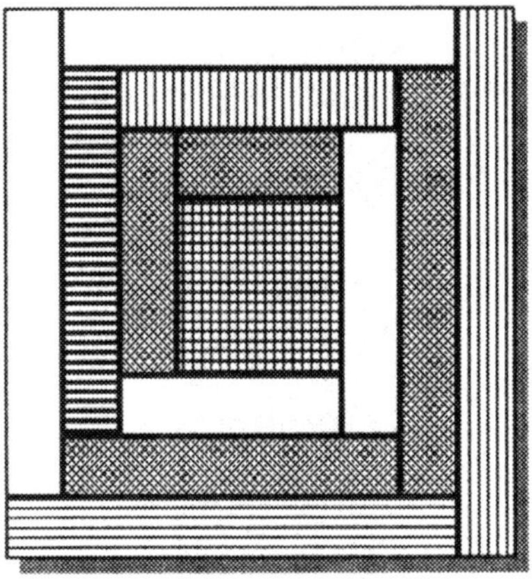

## *Simple Designs for Block Rugs*

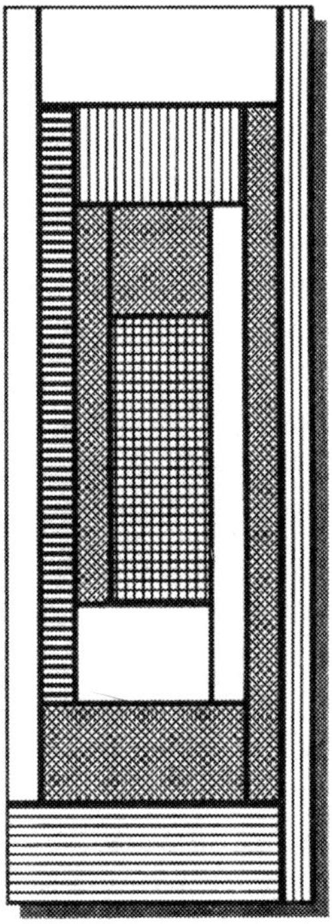

*The Log Cabin (above) is assembled in order going around the center square. This design is familiar because of the quilt pattern of the same name, but it can also be modified to make long runner rugs such as the example at right.*

*Below is another option for simple block assembly which is begun by kniting the four center blocks and assembling them at right angles.*

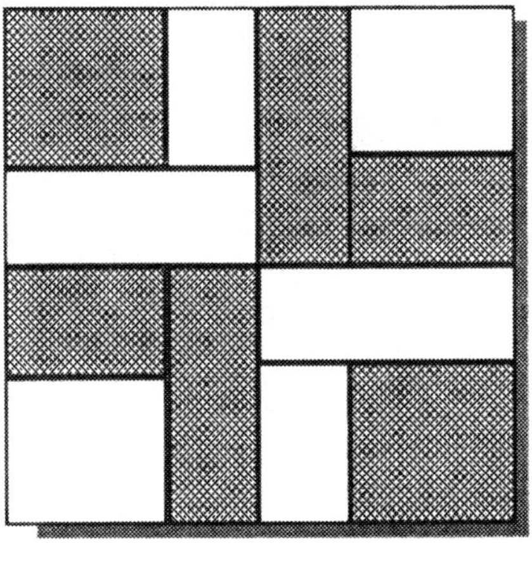

For All Three 24" X 36" Rug Designs Shown on the Facing Page
Fabric Required:
Using torn 1 inch strips of light cotton—allow 8 yards of fabric (45 inches wide)
Using cut and double-folded strips 1½ inches wide of light cotton—allow 11½ to 12 yards of woven cotton fabric (45 inches wide)
Using cotton T-shirt fabric (60 inches wide) cut into 1 inch strip—allow 8½ yards

All rugs are knitted on Size 15 (10mm) needles, using the garter stitch throughout. Each rug is knitted in three strips. Each strip is 16 stitches wide and 96 rows long.
Cast on 16 stitches
Slip 1, Knit 15
Continue until 96 rows are completed and cast off.
(Note the color changes in the individual rug designs below.)

RUG 'A': SIMPLE STRIPES (shown at upper left)
Each stripe uses 1/3 of the fabric total for the type of fabric you are using. These can be made of two dark fabrics and one light or medium tone three different fabrics.

RUG 'B': CHECKERBOARD (shown at lower left)
Slightly less than half of the fabric should be of a dark color and slightly more than half of a light color. This is a awkward to estimate so just divide the fabric required in half and allow a 10% extra of light. Knit two (outer) strips with 32 rows of light, then 32 rows of dark, then 32 rows of light fabric. Knit one (center) strip with 32 rows of dark, then 32 rows of light, then 32 rows of dark fabric.

RUG 'C': SIMPLE CROSS (shown at lower right)
Slightly less than half of the fabric should be of a light color and slightly more than half of a dark color. This is awkward to estimate so just divide the fabric required in half and allow a 10% extra of dark. Knit two (outer) strips with 32 rows of light, then 32 rows of dark, then 32 rows of light fabric. Knit one center strip with only the darker fabric.

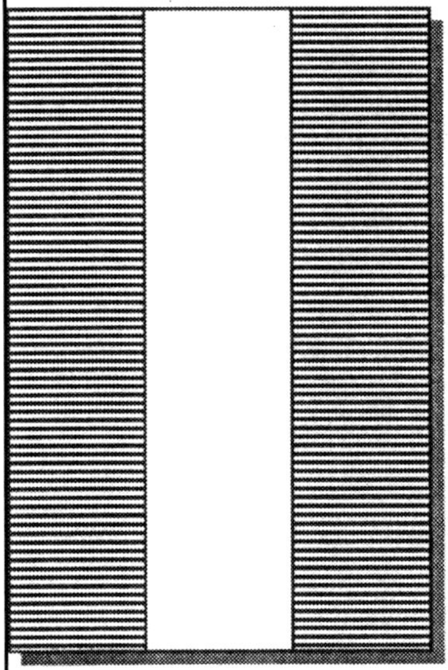

## *Simple Designs for Strip Rugs Using Just Two Colors of Fabric*

*All three of these rugs are 24 x 36 inches and knitted in three strips, each eight inches wide. Allow 12 yards of 45-inch cotton fabric for each rug. Note how differently each rug appears simply because of the arrangement of the light and dark fabrics.*

*Stripes will visually elongate the rug, while the cross will make the rug appear wider. With the checkerboard, notice that the lighter fabric in the center tends to enlarge it.*

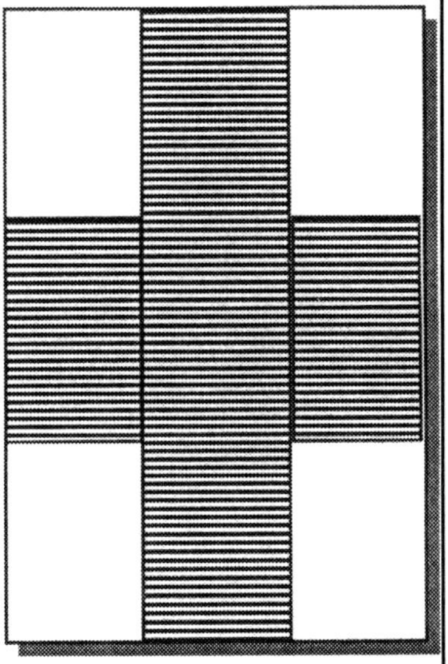

**Estimating the width of your knitted strips or blocks.**

You are not limited to any standard width in a knitted rug. In one rug, you can combine knitted strips or blocks of several different widths to enhance your design. If you are working toward an exact measurement—for example your rug has to be exactly 29 inches wide—knit a test section with your fabric of choice and measure it to determine the precise gauge.

**Putting Your Rug Together**

The lacing process for a "strip" rug is done after all of the strips are knitted. For a "block" rug, lace each piece to the rug as it is completed. If you used the garter stitch or the shingle pattern to knit your rug, it isn't necessary to block the strips before they are joined. If you used a stockinette stitch, rug assembly will be easier if you steam the knitted sections flat before joining.

**Step 1:** Lay the knitted rug sections on the floor in the order they will appear in the rug. You will find that some knitted sections have a better side, or appear differently when turned the opposite direction. When you are satisfied with the layout, pin notes to each strip reminding you of the strip placement.

**Step 2:** Decide which fabric to use for joining. You should have fabric strip left over from the knitting. If your rug contains two contrasting colors of strip that will be joined together, choose the darker or duller color for the joining. Cut a length of strip one-and-one-half times as long as the seam for lacing together the two knitted sections.

**Step 3:** Lace the knitted sections together. Thread the fabric strip into a lacing or weaving needle with a large eye. (Lacking a lacing needle, use a safety pin on the end of the strip for the lacing to use as a needle.) Pin the end of the fabric strip to one end of the knitting leaving about six inches to lace back into the work later.

Insert the lacing needle into the very first loop of the knitting in the corner of one of the knitted sections to be joined. Bring the needle up through the back of the corresponding loop on the other knitted section. Repeat this process to make a snug joint.

Make one whip stitch through both corresponding knitted loops at the ends of the first rows of knitting. Then use one whip stitch to join the second rows of knitting. Continue lacing the ends of corresponding rows until the entire seam is completed.

The lacing should be very snug, so that the sections are firmly joined together, but not so tight that the strips are distorted. Put two whip stitches in the last knitted row, and cut off the fabric strip so about six inches remain.

Repeat this lacing process until all knitted sections are joined. After all of the sections are put together, lay the rug flat on the floor to check that the lacing is not so tight that it keeps the rug from laying flat. Loosen the lacing if necessary.

**Step 4:** Lace in all ends of fabric strip. You will have several little tails of fabric strip that need to be worked into the rug to finish it—from casting on, casting off and the lacing. Use the same lacing needle as for joining and work these tag ends into the knitting. Sew the ends in place with needle and thread, and clip off any excess very close to the work.

**Edging a Strip or Block Rug.** There are several edge finishes that can be used to accent and/or stablilize a strip or block style knitted rug. With the garter stitch or any of the other "structural" patterns, edging isn't really necessary—just a matter of taste. With the stockinette stitch and its relatives, an edging is necessary to prevent curling when the rug is in use. See the Handbook section for the various types of techniques that can be used for edging the finished rug.

CHAPTER 4

# *Knitting a Shaggy Rug*

There are several different ways to achieve a shaggy appearance in a knitted rug. The fluff mat was published in the 1920s but probably dates back into the late 1800s. Examples of the strung shag have been estimated to date from the mid-1800s. The strung shag is an awkward and slow process combining both yarn and scrap fabric, but I'm including it here since you may be curious to try it. The other methods are the result of my own experiments.

With the recent popularity of shaggy rug surfaces, I was pretty sure there had to be a quicker way to achieve the same result in knitted rugs and create a more durable rug in the process. The only two existing methods combined yarn and rag pieces, but I was looking for all-fabric alternatives, which would make a more durable rug. The first three of the rug variations are the result and all can be machine-washed.

**Shaggy Knit Rug #1 with Sewn Joinings:** The first way to knit a shaggy is by using a simple modification in the way the fabrics are prepared. This type of rug is very effective if a lot of different fabrics are used, so it is ideal for using up sewing scraps and old clothing. Try to use just one type of fabric—an all-calico rug is very vintage looking or a T-shirt rug is very soft and fun.

Tear woven cotton fabrics into 1-inch strips, or cut T-shirt fabrics into 1-inch strips. Each strip should be between 8 and 16 inches long. The shorter the strips, the denser the shags on the surface. Strips longer than 16 inches will create only a very sparse look in the finished rug. The torn strips can be all the same length or random lengths within that range.

To sew the strips together for knitting, match the ends of two strips and sew across at the height that you desire for the shaggy surface of the rug. Seams about two inches from the ends of the strips will

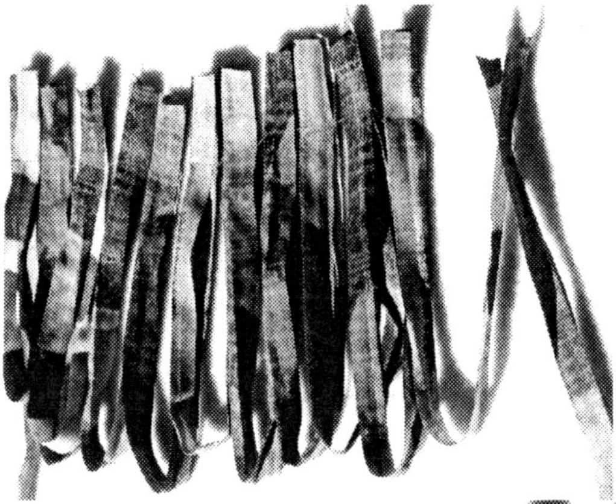

*Above, several 10-inch strips are sewn together with seams about two inches from the ends. At right, is a detail view with the seams highlighted. Sewing several sections, one after another, is the fastest method to sew the strips.*

create a shag texture two inches long. That is a good height for most light cotton fabrics.

If you have a lot of different fabrics, try to mix them up very well as you sew to get the most blended appearance in the rug. Of course, you can use just a single color of fabric for a solid color in the finished rug, or you can group fabrics so that you end up with blocks of color.

These shaggy rugs are most easily made as strip rugs just as in Chapter 2. If you are using very lightweight fabrics, use the garter stitch directions so that the rug has extra softness underfoot. For most fabrics though, the stockinette stitch is preferable since the rug lays a little flatter. Whichever stitch you use, try not to get the shag ends caught in the stitch itself. If you can't make a particular shag face the right direction as you are knitting, you can always pull those ends to the proper side with a small crochet hook after the knitting itself is done.

I haven't specified any particular number of stitches for the knitted sections. You can knit narrow or wide sections, but don't cast on so many stitches that you overfill the needles. Use Size 15 (10 mm) needles 14 inches long or circular

**Garter stitch shaggy rug:**

Cast on desired number of stitches

Slip 1, Knit across

Repeat until knitting reaches desired length, then cast off stitches

Try to hold all of the loose shag ends to one side of the rug as you work.

***Above is a stockinette rug shown in progress. Note that all of the shags are turned to the other side of the rug, so that the stockinette texture is visible on the rug's underside.***

**Stockinette stitch shaggy rug**

Cast on desired number of stitches

Slip 1, Knit across, holding the shag ends to the back of the work (away from you)

Slip 1, Purl across, holding the shag ends to the front of the work (toward you)

Repeat alternate Knit and Purl rows until knitting reaches desired length, then cast off stitches.

When you have knitted as many sections as you want for your rug, it is time to lace the sections together. Take several of the fabric strips that were set aside and join them into a length using the overlapping bias joint (see Chapter 2 or Handbook section). You'll want a strip for lacing that is about twice as long as the knitted sections to be joined. Lace the sections together using a whip stitch following the directions for strip and block rugs in Chapter 3. Leave a tail of about six inches at the beginning of the lacing and at the end of the lacing to weave back into the rug.

Take a look at your finished rug on the floor. If you see any particularly bare spots where the shags are thinner than the rest of the rug, you can fill them in. Using a lacing needle or crochet hook, pull a section of strip under a knitted stitch and make a few stitches by hand to sew it in place. Clip it off even with the other shags.

If you decide your rug is too shaggy, you can simply trim the shag ends down to a shorter length—even as short as ½ inch above the knitting.

**Shaggy Rug #1 without Sewing:** This rug is constructed just like the previous rug, but the fabric strip is prepared without any sewing involved. Instead the strips are joined using one of the "slit and loop" methods called the "bow tie joint" or "bow tie joining." This type of joining is simple to learn, but does take a little practice to do evenly. The resulting rug will not be as smooth underfoot as the sewn type, but is almost as durable a long as the rug isn't abused.

Cut or tear the strips for the rug 1-inch to 1½ -inches wide (choose one width for the rug) and 6 to 16 inches long. At both ends

## *The "Bow Tie" Joint (for shaggy rug #1, without sewing)*

*Cut small slits in the ends of the strips to be joined. The slits should only be just large enough to allow the strip to pass through.*

*Pass the end of the old strip through the slit in the new strip.*

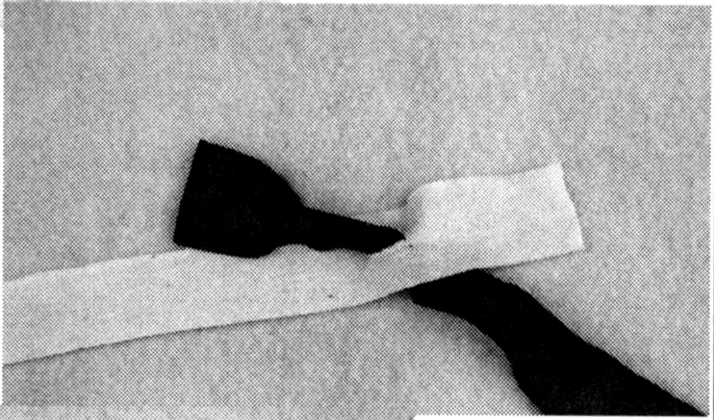

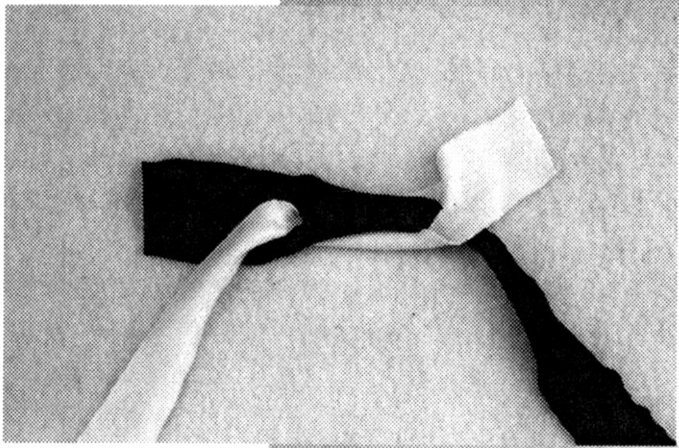

*Then pass the end of the new strip through the slit in the old strip.*

*Tighten the joint by pulling the strips gently. (You'll see how the bowtie joint got its name.*

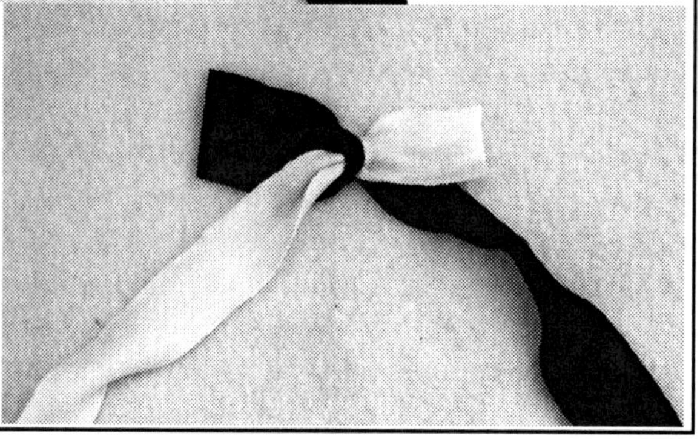

of each strip clip a tiny slit 2 inches from the end. The slit should be as small as possible—just large enough for another strip to pass through.

Insert the end of the first strip into the slit in the second strip. Then insert the end of the second strip through the slit in the first strip. (See illustration.) Pull gently to tighten the knot and raise the shaggy ends up from the strip.

The rug is then knitted and finished using the directions above. As you knit, try to keep all of the shag ends to the same side of the rug. If some don't cooperate, ignore them until the knitting is completed. Then use a small crochet hook to pull the ends to the proper side. (Note that the "bow tie joining" can be used for un-shaggy rugs also. See the Handbook section for details.)

**Shaggy Knit Rug #2:** For this knitted rug, you'll need to prepare one fabric as the "base" for knitting by tearing or cutting your strips and then joining it into a continuous length with the overlapping bias joint. Once the base fabric is ready, the "shags" are sewn directly to it. The advantage of using this type of preparation is that it allows you more control to plan colors and even to use fabrics for the shags that wouldn't work for the knitting. For example, a very fancy rug can be made with velvet, denim or wool snippets. These fabrics don't knit up for beans, but they will make shags. The base fabric for a rug with those sorts of fabrics would be a good quality cotton broadcloth or knit.

The first step is to select the fabric that you want to use for your shags that will form the surface of the rug. Unlike other knitted rugs, there aren't any limits with this one as to the type of fabric that can be used. Shiny metallics, ultra-suede, old jeans, wool coats, silk—just about anything that can be sewn on your sewing machine. It can be knit, open-weave, felted or any other surface texture. If the fabrics you've chosen for the shag tend to ravel, cut them on the bias. For a shag that is one inch high all over the rug, cut the shag pieces 2 inches long, and one inch wide. Light fabrics for shags can be cut 2 inches square and folded over lengthwise to increase their body.

Then select the fabric you want to actually knit with as the base fabric. The base fabric will act as a background color to widely spaced shags, but will be mostly invisible if you place your shag pieces closely. The base fabric can be a woven cotton or blend fabric or cotton t-shirt knit. The only real limit on the base fabric is that it must hold the sewing stitches firmly, so avoid delicate, loosely-woven or open-weave fabrics. Cut (or tear) the base fabric into strips one inch wide, and join all of these strips together using the overlapping bias joint. Once the base fabric is prepared, the shags are added to it.

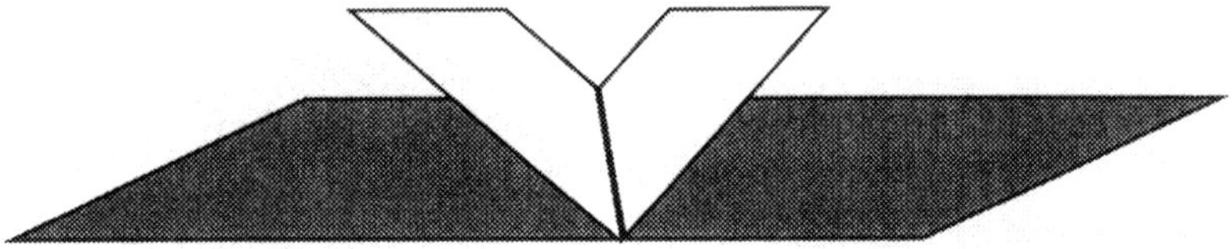

Fold a shag piece in half, and sew the middle of the shag piece directly to the base fabric, as illustrated above. Then move along the base fabric and sew another shag about every 6 to 10 inches. If you cut the shag pieces into two-inch squares, fold them in half before sewing to the base fabric. Sew shags the entire length of your prepared base fabric.

With this type of fabric preparation, it helps to knit a test section to see how you like your shag placement before all of your shag pieces are sewn onto the base. Look at the sample piece to see if you need to adjust the shag spacing. If you want your shag to be denser, space the pieces more closely. If you want it less dense, space the pieces a little farther apart.

Another nice effect that is made possible with this type of preparation is to use fabrics of two very different colors. The base fabric becomes the background for the shags. For example, a base fabric of brown broadcloth could serve as the back ground for shags of

a calico in a mix of autumn tones, giving the effect of autumn leaves. Or if you really want to be bold use something like electric blue as the base fabric and brilliant orange or hot pink as the shags. The warmer colors will appear to float on the background.

Follow the same knitting, assembly and finishing directions as for the Shaggy Knit Rug #1.

**Shaggy Rug #3 (A Vintage Fluff Mat):** This type of shaggy knit rug uses a yarn as the rug base. In the introduction are the complete 1927 directions for this type of rug and a photo of one. Unlike many vintage directions, Mrs. Bowles are clear enough to follow. She directs that the shags be inserted every third stitch which was to try to keep tension on the yarn. In fact however, a better rug is made by inserting a shag piece in each stitch across. All you have to do is keep in mind that tension counts and give the yarn a light tug to tighten it over each shag piece. In this type of knitted rug, working tightly is actually a virtue, since the tighter the stitches, the more snugly the shag pieces are held into the rug.

Any type of tightly spun yarn of medium weight can be used for a fluff mat, and should be matched to the type of fabric that is used for the shags. For example, if you are going to use wool fabric for the shag surface, choose a worsted weight wool yarn to act as the base. Likewise, with cotton/blend fabrics use a cotton yarn.

Because the shag scraps are so small, this is a good method for recycling clothing. T-shirts, sweatshirts, old jeans or skirts will all yield quite a lot of scrap. This type of rug will be most durable with a resilient fabric that the yarn can really sink into with each stitch. Remember that it is only the friction of the yarn on the fabric piece that holds it in place.

Cut knit fabrics lengthwise or cross-wise ¾ to 1 inch wide (narrower for heavier knits like sweatshirts). Cut woven fabrics on the bias in the same width range (¾ inch for old jeans to 1 inch for light shirtings). The shags should be twice as long as you want the height of the shag in the finished rug. A good length to cut them is 3 inches yielding a 1½-inch shag. Pieces cut less than 2 inches long can be hard to handle and keep evenly placed. When the rug is completed, you can trim the shags shorter, but since all that is holding the shags in place is the friction of the yarn they really shouldn't be trimmed to less than one inch high.

The rug can be knitted with either the garter stitch or the stockinette stitch and it is recommended that you knit a small test sample using the yarn and shag pieces for the rug. The directions call for using a size 10 knitting needle, but if your yarn or fabrics are particularly light in weight smaller needles may be needed to create a firm texture. Test the firmness by tugging lightly on a shag piece to see if it resists pulling out of the knitting. If it comes out fairly easily, switch to smaller needles.

This type of shaggy rug is most suited to a simple strip rug assembly, but can be knitted in a single piece or used in a round or oval coil knitted rug. The procedure in handling each piece of shag does slow down the knitting process somewhat so more complex stitches or patterns (such as the wedge) are really not a good idea.
The knitting (garter stitch) proceeds as follows:

- Cast on the desired number of stitches with the yarn.

- Slip 1, Knit across. Repeat for a second row.

- On the third row, you will begin inserting the shags on the third stitch. So, slip the first stitch and knit the second stitch. Then, fold the shag piece across the yarn. Insert the right needle into the stitch on the left needle just as for a normal knit stitch. When you bring the yarn over the needles to complete the knit stitch, the shag piece should be caught up in the stitch itself. Keep your work tight. After each stitch with a shag inserted, tug on the yarn to take up any slack.

- Continue across the row, inserting one shag in each stitch and keeping the ends of the shags to the back side of the work. The last two stitches are knitted without a shag inserted.

## *Shaggy Rug #4: How to "knit in" shag pieces*

*Above is a vintage fluff mat in progress, which has the beginning rows already worked and is at the point of starting a new row in which shags will be added. Note that the first and second stitches are already on the right needle, since they do not have added shags.*

*In the upper right of the photo, a shag piece is folded over the yarn, ready to slide up next to the needle. The stitch is then completed as if it were a normal stitch and the shag piece is caurght up into the stitch by the action of the yarn.*

*Because only friction is holding the shag piece in place, you may need to tug lightly on the yarn after each stitch to maintain the proper tension. The completed stitch is shown at right.*

- The fourth row is done only with the yarn (no shags at all). Slip 1, Knit across.
- Repeat the third and fourth rows alternately to complete the shaggy section of the rug.
- Finish off the rug with two rows of knitting with the yarn only (Slip 1, Knit across) and then cast off the stitches.

If you made several sections of knitted shag, you will need to join them to form the finished rug. The knitted sections can be laced together or crocheted together using the same yarn as used for the knitting. If crocheting, use a hook with the same diameter as the knitting needles. A chain stitch is easiest and has the advantage of a little bit of stretch that will help the base to lie flat.

Note that most knitting yarns are not very resistant to abrasion and can be slippery on a hardwood or tile floor. It is recommended that an expanded rubber mat be used under these sorts of rugs to minimize both problems. No mat is needed if the rug is used over carpeting.

Of all of the types of shaggy rugs, these are the most delicate. These rugs should not be machine-washed. Hand washing in the bathtub is preferred. Just be sure to rinse the rug completely to remove any traces of soap, let excess water drain off, and then press the rug between two large towels to remove as much moisture as possible. Use your hands to lightly ruffle up the shag pieces and then let the rug dry flat.

**Shaggy Rug #4, A Strung Shag Rug:** There are examples of strung shag rugs from the mid- and late 1800s and they are easy to spot since they often recycled not only clothing but leftover pieces of string as well. It is not unusual to find one of these rugs with many different colors and types of string used in the base. Knitted strung shag rugs were more common than crocheted (from the surviving examples) and it is fairly easy to distinguish the two by examining the back side of the rug, since the knit stitches or the crochet stitches show distinctly.

The advantage of the strung shag rug over the fluff mat (Shaggy Rug #3) is that the shag bits of fabric are actually secured by sewing through them, so they can't pull out. The disadvantage is that the working yarn has to be broken and re-attached regularly which can be a nuisance.

These rugs need a base of good quality yarn with a fiber content matching the fabric used for the shag pieces. If you are using cotton (or blend) fabrics, yarns such as the Sugar 'n Cream brand are a good choice. With wool fabrics, a quality worsted weight yarn should be used. With synthetic materials a tightly spun synthetic yarn can be used or a cotton yarn.

Because the shag scraps are so small, this is a good method for recycling clothing. T-shirts, sweatshirts, old jeans or skirts will all yield quite a lot of scrap. Cut knit fabrics lengthwise or cross-wise ¾ to 1 inch wide (narrower for heavier knits like sweatshirts). Cut woven fabrics on the bias in the same width range (¾ inch for old jeans to 1 inch for light shirtings). The shags should be twice as long as you want the height of the shag in the finished rug. A good length to cut them is 3 inches yielding a 1½ inch shag. When the rug is completed, you can trim the shags shorter if you like.

I always recommend making a practice piece with the yarn and fabric of your choice since your taste in shagginess may be different than mine. If you want your rug to be fuller than your practice piece, you can cut the shag fabrics a little wider or move to a little smaller sizeof knitting needles.

Thread an embroidery needle, or small tapestry needle with the yarn. The needle should have the smallest eye that will accept the yarn. Insert the needle in the center of the shag piece and slide the shag piece down the thread. Then string another and another until

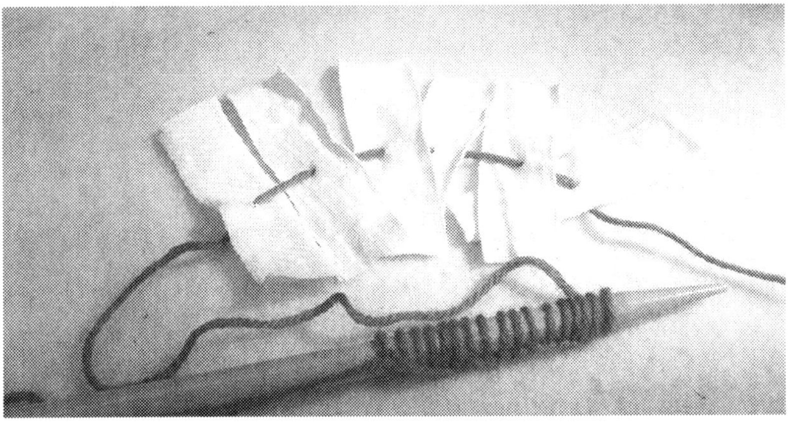

you have a collection of a couple dozen shags strung onto the thread. Don't put on too many or you won't be able to slide them along without a lot of struggle. How many to string on at one time will depend on how heavy the fabric is and how many stitches you are going to put in a row.

**Directions:** Use size 15 (10 mm) knitting needles and cast on 10 or 12 stitches for your first practice piece or as many as you like for your rug—just don't overfill the needles. Slide the shag pieces down the thread far enough to be able to cast on the desired number of stitches. Then begin the first row of knitting.

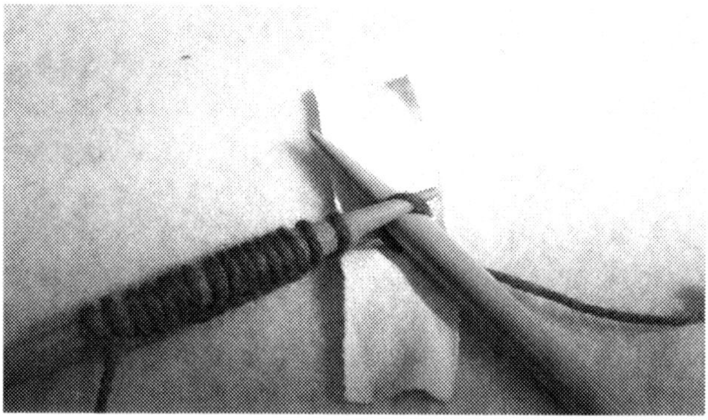

Insert the empty knitting needle into the first stitch to be knitted. Slide one shag up the string until it just touches the needle. Knit one. Insert the needle into the next stitch, slide the next shag up the string and knit a second stitch. Keep on with the same procedure, always making sure to keep the shags to the back of the work as you knit the first row.

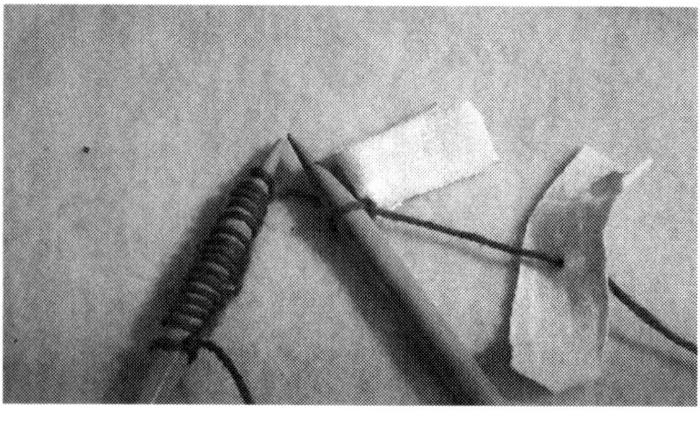

The second row is done by purling, forming the stockinette stitch. I prefer the stockinette stitch for these rugs because the ends of the shag pieces can be held alternately to the two sides of the work and so does the yarn. It is just a more natural feel in the work to alternate knit and purl rows along with switching the shag ends to the back and front with each row.

To begin the second row, slide a shag piece up the thread, purl the first stitch and repeat across the row. On this second row, the shags should all be turned to the front of the work (toward you).

The third row repeats the first knitted row and the fourth row is purled across. The work continues just alternating knitted and purled rows.

Sooner or later you'll run out of shag pieces to incorporate into the stitching. When you do, cut the yarn 3 or 4 yards from the last stitch and thread the free end (attached to the knitting) into the embroidery or tapestry needle. Thread on a whole bunch more shags. (You should have a feel for how your shag pieces will act now, so you can thread on as many as you think will handle fairly easily.) Then continue knitting. If you run out of shags before you run out of yarn, just thread more on.

When there is only about 3 inches of yarn left, stop knitting and tie on a new section of yarn 3, 4 or 5 yards long. Tie the knot very close to the last stitch that you made.

A simple overhand knot with the yarn ends usually works the best. Don't cut off the thread ends though. They will be worked back into the shags using the tapestry or embroidery needle. Just run the needle through several knitted stitches until the end of the thread disappears into the work. (I usually wait until there are quite a few sets of thread ends dangling before I do this. It seems more efficient if you can deal with several at once.)

Then thread more shag pieces on the other end of the yarn, slide them up to the work and continue knitting. Continue making rows with the practice piece until you are comfortable with the process of knitting around the shag pieces and knotting off the thread. If you are knitting a sample piece, take a look at the texture. If you want a tighter spacing of your shag pieces, switch to a smaller size pair of needles for the rug or cut your shag pieces a little wider.

Strung shag knitting is the most efficient if you can knit the rug in one piece on a pair of circular needles. (See the Handbook

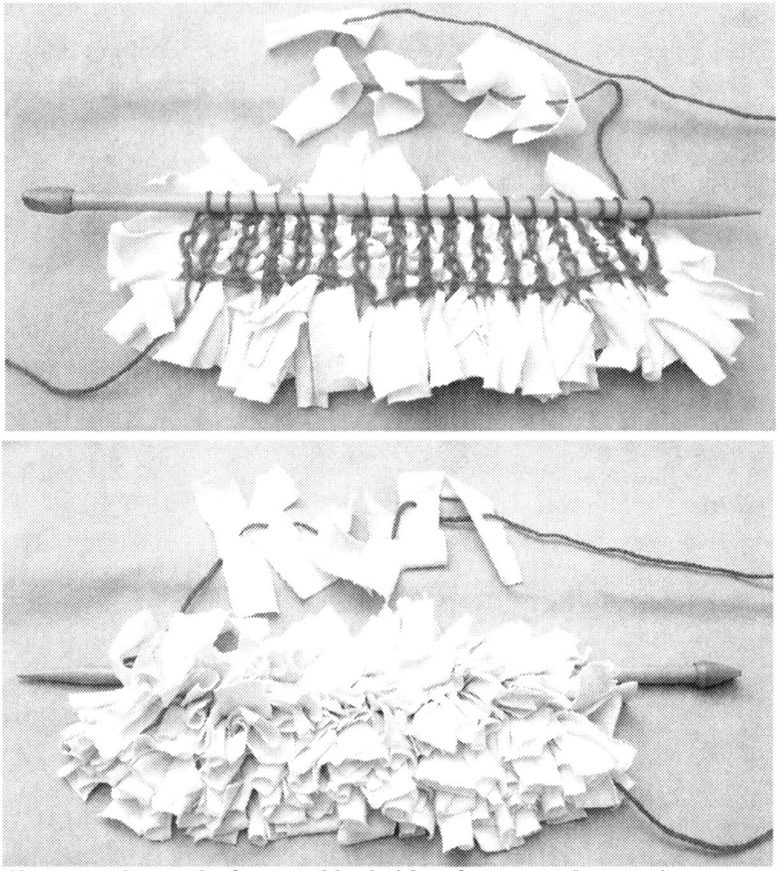

***Above are shown the front and back sides of a strung shag rug in progress. Using a contrasting color of yarn, the stockinette stitch on the reverse of the rug is plain. The front of the rug shows the density of shags made from 3/4-inch cotton T-shirt fabric.***

section for how to make your own if you can't find circular needles in the right size.) Also, before you begin your rug, take a look at your sample piece to determine the gauge (how many stitches to the inch) so that you know how many stitches you'll need to cast on for the rug size that you want.

**For a rug:** String a collection of shag pieces onto the working thread, then cast on the desired number of stitches. Slide a shag up next to the needle and knit the first stitch. Slide the next shag up the string and knit the second stitch. Continue across the row in the same manner. Keep all shags turned to the back side of the work. Turn the work and slide a shag up to the needle, then purl the first stitch. Continue across the row in the same manner incorporating one shag in each stitch. Keep all shags turned to the front of the work. Tie on more yarn as needed in lengths of three to five yards at a time.

It is a real mess to try to cast off with a shag in the middle of things so when your rug reaches the desired size, cast off just using the yarn making sure that your tension is loose enough to not pucker the end. Use the embroidery needle to work the cut ends of the yarn into the knitting.

If you used washable yarn and washable fabric for the shags, this type of rug will be machine washable (gentle cycle of course) and the shag ends should be protected from snagging. Wash the rug inside a large net bag, or hand wash it in the bath tub like the fluff mat. Don't hang it to dry since the weight of the wet rug will cause the yarn to stretch. Lay the rug flat instead and ruffle up the shags gently with your hands. Let the rug dry completely before using.

## Shaggy Rug Techniques that are a Waste of Time

There are a couple of other ways of knitting a shaggy rug that were published after World War II and neither is very practical. In the first, a piece of scrap fabric is laid between two stitches, then a stitch is knit, and finally the other end of the scrap is moved to the back side of the rug and the next stitch is knit. The scrap pieces handled that way will pull out of the rug with very little pressure. The method was probably written up by someone that had seen one of the earlier "fluff mats" (see Shaggy Rug #3) but really didn't understand its construction.

The second method to avoid was clearly influenced by the popularity of latch hooking in the 1950s. Basically these directions are to knit a yarn base for the rug and then go back and use a latch hook or rug hook to attach yarns or fabric scraps to the knitting. My assessment is that it is a lot quicker just to make a latch hook rug on a standard latch hook canvas base than to knit something just to latch hook onto.

CHAPTER 5:

# *An Introduction to Knitting in the Round*

While strip and block rugs can be made with many different stitch patterns, round knitted rugs have historically been made using the basic garter stitch almost exclusively. This is because the round shape requires the built-in stretch of the garter stitch that allows knitted sections to bend into curves. Alternate stitches can be used for the outer rounds as the diameter of the rug increases and the knitted strips do not have to bend as much as in the center of a rug.

In making a round knitted rug, the joining of the rug seams or sections is as critical as the knitting. Sections of round rugs are always joined with lacing and each round is laced as it is completed. Round rugs can be knitted in three distinct ways. Each method offers its own design considerations and potentials. All three of these methods can also be used for oval rugs, but only the bullseye and the wedge patterns can be modified to make half-round rugs.

## Coiled Construction: One Long Knitted Section

The easiest method for knitting a round rug is the coiled construction. The beginning and ending of the knitting is tapered but the body of the rug is formed by a long section of straight garter stitching. The coiled construction has a limited range of design possibilities and is actually the most effective when made in either a solid color or a hit or miss pattern with dozens of different colors and prints used in the rug. Because the rug can be ended at any point, you don't need to worry about exact yardages, and the technique lends itself well to recycling clothing.

## *Techniques for Creating Round and Oval Knitted Rugs*

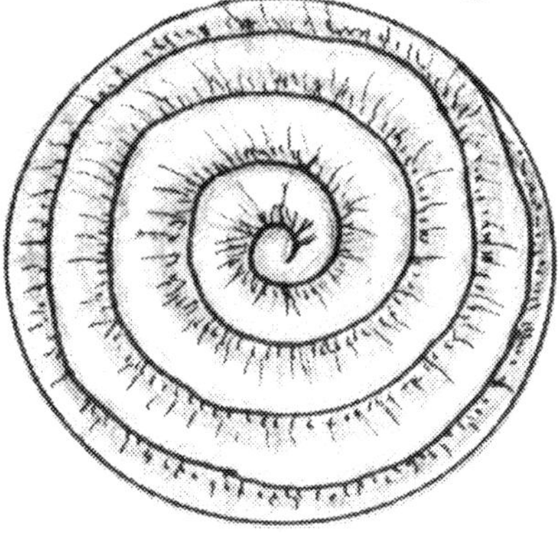

*Coiled knitting is made in one continuous section which is curled around on itself. The coil can only be made with flexible stitches, such as the garter stitch.*

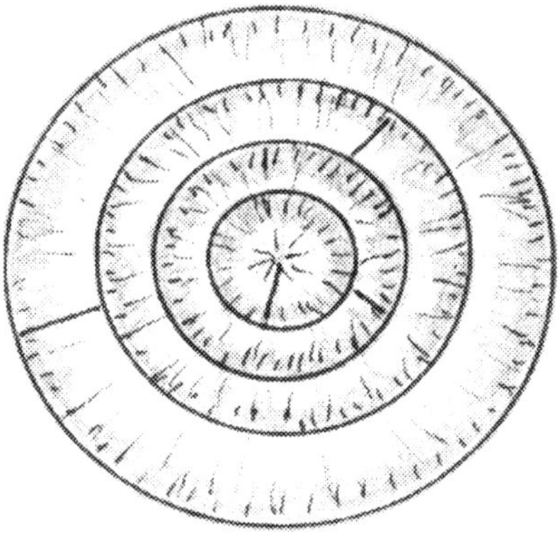

*Bullseye rugs are made by knitting a round center section and adding bands of knitting to the outside edge. The rounds of knitting can be of various widths.*

*Wedge knitted rugs are knit in a single piece. The shape is made by using partial rows in series, with each set forming one wedge.*

**Wedge Knitting: Circular Rugs Knitted in a Single Section**

The second technique is wedge knitting. This method allows you to create round and half-round rugs. Wedges are formed by knitting a progression of partial rows. The wedge pattern lends itself to a variety of designs, but the most often used is the old-fashioned "fan" design where each wedge is knitted from a different color. Additional rounds of knitting can be added to wedge knitted rugs in the same manner as the bullseye.

**Bullseye Knitting: A Round Center with Garter Bands Set in Rings**

The third method of round knitting is the "target" or "bullseye" pattern. This method combines a round center with bands of garter stitching surrounding the center. The ends of these outer bands are butted together to match exactly. Each round is a separate unit creating the bullseye effect.

# CHAPTER 6

# *Coil Knitted Rugs*

First of all—don't be intimidated by the knitting and assembly instructions. They look complex to a beginning knitter, but taken one step at a time, a coil knitted rug is really very simple. In fact, round and oval coil knitted rugs are an excellent choice for a first rug.

The center of the rug is knitted beginning with only two stitches. The knitting gradually increases to eight stitches wide at Row 85. The knitting is then a straight strip of garter stitching until the rug gets close to its finished size. In the final rounds of knitting, the width of the knitting gradually decreases again to maintain the round shape or the rounded end of an oval.

As coiled rugs are made, the lacing follows fairly closely behind. The instructions for lacing follow the knitting directions. Note that in the photos, the rugs are shown as they look before lacing. That is simply to illustrate the structure of the rugs—not how the rug itself should be handled.

A coiled knit rug can be made very large—if you have the ambition for the project—even up to room size. Start with a small 24-inch round rug before you start a large one, since your knitting will improve with a little practice. A 24-inch rug will require about 7½ yards of 45-inch wide woven cotton fabric, cut into 1½ inch strips, sewn with the regular bias joint, and double-folded *or* 6 yards of fabric cut or torn into 1 inch strips, joined with the overlapping bias joint and left unfolded.

If using knit fabric, allow about 5¼ yards of 60-inch wide single-knit cotton T-shirt fabric, cut into 1-inch strips and sewn together with the regular bias joint. If you are using up sewing leftovers or recycled clothing, don't be too concerned about how many yards you have. Cut a selection of fabrics and start knitting.

For large rugs you can estimate the yardage you will need by the square foot. Each square foot of rug will require about 2 yards of 45-inch fabric or about 1-1/3 yards of 60-inch knit fabric.

**Round Coil Knitted Rug**

Directions:
Use Size 15 (10mm) knitting needles, 14 inches long.

Cast on 2 stitches.
Row 1: Knit 2
Row 2: Slip 1, Knit 1
Rows 3 through 12: Repeat Rows 1 and 2
Row 13: Knit 1, Cast on 1 stitch, Knit 1
Row 14: Slip 1, Knit 2
Row 15: Knit 3
Row 16: Slip 1, Knit 2
Row 17: Knit 3
Row 18: Slip 1, Knit 2
Row 19: Knit 1, Cast on 1 stitch, Knit 2
Row 20: Slip 1, Knit 3
Row 21: Knit 4
Rows 22 through 26: Repeat Rows 20 and 21 alternately

(Note that all even numbered rows begin with a Slip, and all odd numbered rows begin with a Knit. This helps to create a natural curve in the knitting.)

Row 27: Knit 1, Cast on 1 Stitch, Knit 3
Row 28: Slip 1, Knit 4
Row 29: Knit 5
Rows 30 through 40: Repeat rows 28 and 29
(End with a repeat of row 28)

Row 41: Knit 1, Cast on 1 stitch, Knit 4
Row 42: Slip 1, Knit 5
Row 43: Knit 6
Rows 44 through 58: Repeat Rows 42 and 43

## *Assembling a Round Coiled Knitted Rug*

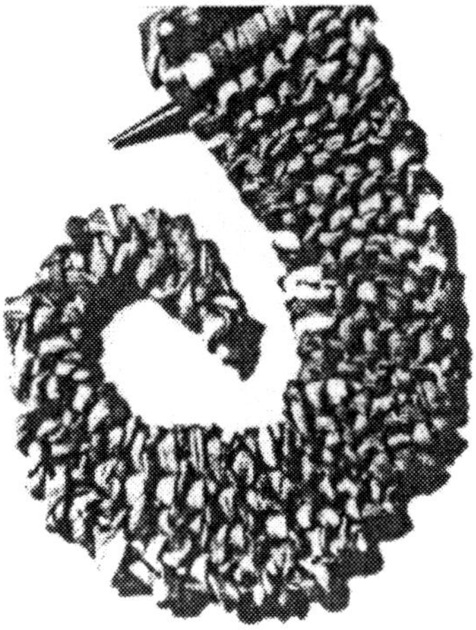

*At left is the beginning section of a round coiled knitted rug, ready to begin lacing.*

*Below, the initial center lacing is completed.*

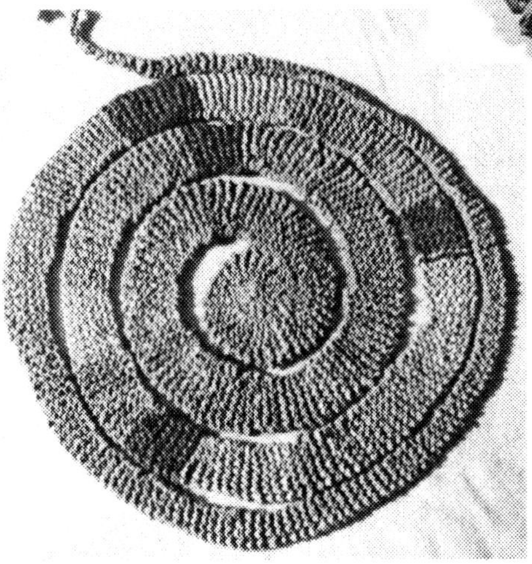

*The round coiled knitted rug showing how the rug goes together. Note how the outermost rounds of knitting are tapered to keep the round shape in the finished rug.*

Row 59: Knit 1, Cast on 1 stitch, Knit 5
Row 60: Knit 7
Rows 62 through 82: Repeat Rows 60 and 61
Row 83: Knit 1, Cast on 1 stitch, Knit 6
Row 84: Slip 1, Knit 7
Row 85: Knit 8

All rows to follow: repeat rows 84 and 85, until the rug is about 6 inches smaller in diameter than the desired size. Then see "ending the rug."

**Assembling the Rug :**

The coiled knitting will be laced into shape using a section of the same fabric strip that you use for the knitting. Cut a section of fabric strip about two feet long and sew one end to the tag of strip at the very beginning of the knitting where you cast on the stitches. Thread the other end into a large-eye lacing needle, tapestry needle or weaving needle. Use a safety pin on the end of the strip if you don't have a suitable needle at hand.

Note that the knitting has a natural curve.This curve is created by the knitting pattern itself. You will be tightening this curve to form the center of the rug. Work on a table so that you can be sure the center lays flat.

Curl the very beginning of the rug, tightening its natural curve until it fits snugly against the rest of the knitting. This is where you will place your first stitch. With a whip stitch, catch the inside loop of the knitting on the outside of the curve and its matching row on the coil. Then follow the curve around, lacing the matching rows together. Lace the knitting snugly so that the spiral lays flat at the center. Ease in the outer rows—do not stretch them or the rug will begin to "cup." As the lacing strip is used up, sew on additional sections of fabric strip to continue the lacing.

**Ending the Rug:**

In order for the rug to have a rounded shape, the knitting must be tapered very gradually at the outside of the rug. To do this two stitches are knitted together in the middle of a knitted row.

Begin tapering the width of the knitted strip when the assembled rug is about six inches smaller than the final size of the finished rug. Decrease the knitting by one stitch, and mark the place with a safety pin. Decrease again at 1/4, 1/2 and 3/4 around the outside edge of the rug, again marking the location of the decreases with safety pins. At the end of the first decrease round, you will have only 4 stitches remaining on the needle. Lace the round to the rug, leaving the safety pins in place to use as reference points.

On the second round at the outside edge, place the three remaining decreases between the decreases in the previous round. When only one stitch remains, do not cast it off. Instead, remove it from the knitting needles, and insert a large (Size N or P) crochet hook. Crochet a chain about a foot long then pull the end of the strip up through the last chain to secure it.

Lace the final round to the rug, including the ending chain. Lace the fabric strip under several stitches and sew it in place. Clip off any excess.

### Oval Coiled Rugs

It is easy to modify the basic procedure for coiled rugs to make the oval shape. First though you have to know the size of the oval rug that you want to make. Subtract the width from the length to get the center measurement. For example if you want to knit a coiled rug that is 5 feet long and three feet wide, the center measurement would be two feet (5 - 3 = 2).

**Directions:**

Use Size 15 (10mm) knitting needles, 14 inches long.

Cast on 4 stitches.
Row 1: Knit 4
Row 2: Slip 1, Knit 3

Continue to repeat row 2 until the knitting measures twice as long as the center measure ***plus*** 3 inches. (In our example above, the center measure was two feet. So this knitted section should measure 4 feet 3 inches long.) When you reach this measurement, mark the row with a safety pin.

For the next rows, which will form one end of the oval, the number of stitches is gradually increased to 8:

Cast on 1, Knit 4
Slip 1, Knit 4
Slip 1, Knit 4
Slip 1, Knit 4
Cast on 1, Knit 5
Slip 1, Knit 5
Slip 1, Knit 5
Slip 1, Knit 5
Cast on 1, Knit 6
Slip 1, Knit 6
Slip 1, Knit 6
Slip 1, Knit 6
Cast on 1, Knit 7
Slip 1, Knit 7

The rest of the rug (until just before the end) is knitted by repeating this last row (Slip 1, Knit 7). At any point now, you can begin lacing the rug together. To do this cut a length of fabric strip about 2 feet long, and thread one end into a large eye lacing needle. Work on a flat surface.

Fold the beginning of the knitting up to meet the safety pin. Gently flatten the curve at the folded section. Beginning at the inside of the curve, lace the two sides together using a back and forth stitch or a whip stitch, and do not skip any rows. When you reach the safety pin, ease the strip around the center, and lace it to the beginning of the knitting, forming a gentle curve.

Then continue lacing each round as it is knitted. The outer knitted band should lay flat, matched row for row along the straight portions of the oval, and eased around the ends of the curve. Do not stretch the knitting around the curves or the rug will cup. Lacing should be done snugly, but not so tightly as to buckle or pucker the knitting. It helps to work on a flat surface as you are doing the lacing.

## *Assembling the Oval Coiled Knitted Rug*

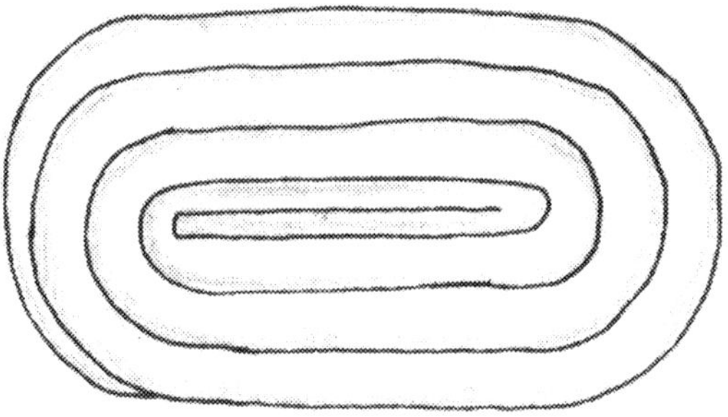

*Above is a sketch of an oval coiled knitted rug showing how the center is formed by a very narrow section, folded back on itself.*

*Below is an oval rug shown in progress, before any lacing has been done. The arrow in the photo pints to the very start of the knitting which forms the center section. If you follow the curve around you will notice that the width of the knitting increases dramatically as it comes past the beginning point on the next round of knitting. This width change is disguised in the finished rug because it occurs on a curve.*

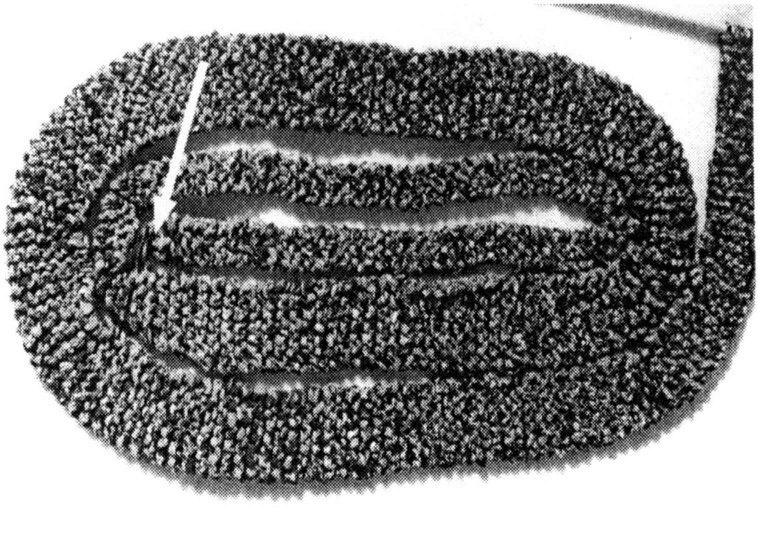

**Ending an oval rug:**

The knitted strip is gradually decreased in width around ***one*** of the end curves. To do this, lace the knitted section to the rug so that you know where to start decreasing. Then estimate how many more rows of knitting it will take to go the rest of the way around the curve. Divide this number by eight. This is how frequently you will decrease by one stitch. For example, if it will take about 72 more rows to finish around the curve, you will decrease the knitting by one stitch in every ninth row.

To decrease, begin a row by knitting two stitches together, instead of making a slip stitch. Mark the decrease row so that you can keep a count for the placement of the next decrease.

When you are down to two stitches and ready for the last decrease, knit the last two stitches together, and use a crochet hook to remove the last loop remaining on the needles. Chain seven or eight stitches, then pull the end of the strip up through the loop. Clip off the remaining strip about 6 inches long.

Then lace the last section around the end of the oval. Work the ends of the fabric strips into the knitting and sew in place. Clip off any excess very close to the surface.

# CHAPTER 7

# *Wedge Knitted Rugs*

The wedge knitted round rug is one of the showiest of the knitted rugs. The radiating effect of the wedges is eye-catching and very appealing. Even when made in a hit-or-miss collection of fabrics, this effect remains. This type of knitted rug can also echo many decorating details—the shape of a fireplace fan, the motif of a quilt or a fan style window.

The wedge knit rug can be made in nearly any size, limited only by the size of your knitting needles. Because you knit the radius, the final diameter will be twice the width of your knitting. For instance, the pattern below for a 24-inch diameter rug can be knitted conveniently on 14-inch needles since the actual width of the knitting is just 12 inches.

To knit larger wedge style rugs, Size 15 (10 mm) circular needles are needed. The longer the needles, the wider you can wedge knit, and the larger the rug you can make in a single piece. Another method of obtaining larger wedge style rugs is to add bands of knitting around the wedge knit center. (See the directions for bullseye rugs in the next chapter if you want to add bands of knitting around a wedge knit center.)

Wedges are made by knitting partial rows. The partial rows are based on two, three, four or more stitches. We'll begin with the two-stitch based wedge since it is the oldest style and was first written about by Amy Mali Hicks in 1914. The two-stitch pattern makes a circle with 12 wedges. I highly recommend that you make the 8-inch or 16-inch practice piece before you proceed with any of the other wedge patterns.

### 8-inch Wedge Knit with a 2-Stitch Repeat

This can be used as a hotpad or as the center of a Bullseye rug.

Use Size 15 (10 mm) needles. Allow ½ yard of cotton fabric if the strips are cut or torn 1 inch wide. Allow ¾ yards of fabric if strips are cut 1½ inches wide and double folded.

**Directions:**

Cast on 8 stitches

Row 1: Knit 2, turn work

Row 2: Slip 1, Knit 1, turn work

Row 3: Knit 4, turn work

Row 4: Slip 1, Knit 3

Row 5: Knit 6, turn work

Row 6: Slip 1, Knit 5

Row 7: Knit 8

Row 8: Slip 1, Knit 7

Rows 1 through 8 make one wedge. Repeat these rows in sequence 12 times to make a full circle.

On the last wedge, don't knit row 8. Cast off as you knit row 7. This will leave the last stitch cast off at the center of the work. Cut the rug strip about 18 inches from the work. You will use this strip to lace the edges of the circle together. Pull the strip end up through the last knitted stitch and lace the end into a large-eye lacing or weaving needle.

Begin lacing the circle by passing the strip under the very center stitches, and pull snug so that the center is closed. Then whip stitch the edges of the circle together. Lace snugly, but don't pull tightly enough to distort the shape of the circle.

### 16-inch Wedge Knit with a 2-Stitch Repeat

This can also be used as a small chairpad or as the center of a bullseye rug.

Use Size 15 (10 mm) needles. Allow 1½ yards of cotton fabric if strips are cut or torn 1 inch wide. Allow 2 yards of fabric if strips are cut 1½ inches wide and double-folded.

**Directions:**

Cast on 16 stitches

Row 1: Knit 2, turn work

Row 2: Slip 1, Knit 1, turn work

## *Round Wedge Knitted Rugs*

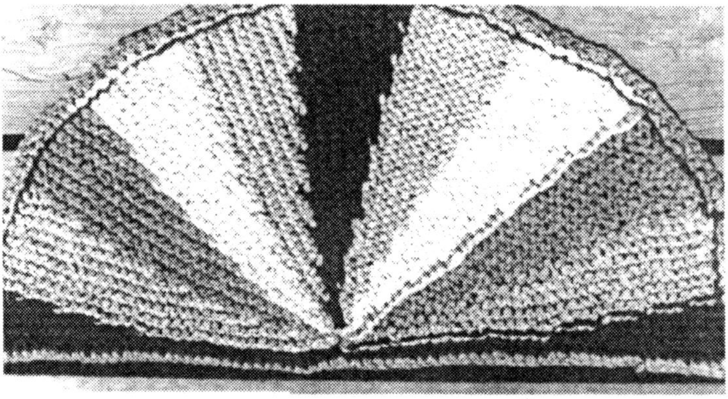

*The showiest wedge knitted rugs include a color change at each wedge. The greater the contrast between the fabrics, the more the wedges will show. Above is a wedge knit rug showing off the fan structure. At right is a wedge rug knitted using a single fabric and the wedges are nearly invisible. Below is a sketch of lacing the center and edges of a wedge knitted rug. (See the text for full directions.)*

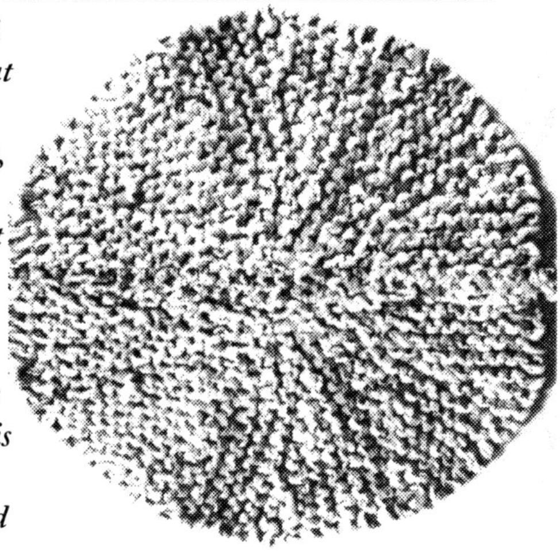

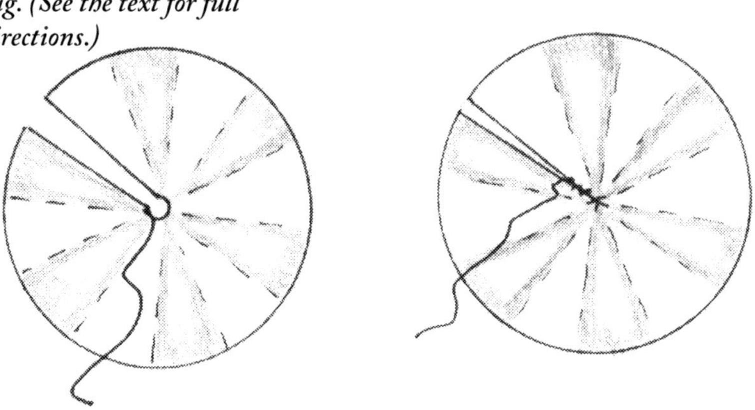

Row 3: Knit 4, turn work
Row 4: Slip 1, Knit 3, turn work
Row 5: Knit 6, turn work
Row 6: Slip 1, Knit 5, turn work
Row 7: Knit 8, turn work
Row 8: Slip 1, Knit 7, turn work
Row 9: Knit 10, turn work
Row 10: Slip 1, Knit 9, turn work
Row 11: Knit 12, turn work
Row 12: Slip 1, Knit 11, turn work
Row 13: Knit 14, turn work
Row 14: Slip 1, Knit 13, turn work
Row 15: Knit 16, turn work
Row 16: Slip 1, Knit 15
Rows 1 through 16 make one wedge. Repeat these rows in sequence 12 times to make a full circle. (Repeat six times to make a half-circle.)

On the last wedge, don't knit row 16, cast off as you knit row 15. Then follow the finishing instructions for the 8-inch center.

**Large Wedge Knit Rugs**

Small round projects like the ones above are knitted by adding two stitches at a time in each pair of rows. These projects require twelve complete wedges to make a full round. However, in the larger knitted projects the two-stitch pattern creates 12 flat sides around the knitting, and the larger the rug gets, the more pronounced these flat sides become. So, to maintain a round shape, larger rugs are knitted in more wedges. A 3-stitch pattern will create a round rug with 18 wedges, a 4-stitch pattern will have about 24 wedges, etc. The more stitches in the repeat, the more wedges will be needed to create a full round. In theory, there isn't a limit to how many stitches can be used in the repeating pattern, up to 1/3 of the total number of stitches that are cast on. (For example, if you cast on 30 stitches, you can knit wedges with up to a 10-stitch repeat.

As a practical matter, larger rugs are most effective using four-stitch repeat in the partial rows, but don't be afraid to experiment with other repeating patterns once you have a little experience with the wedge style of knitting. The wedge knit rug is ideal for using up clothing such as skirts or pants and the small yardages left from sewing projects.

For the 24-inch wedge knitted rug below, allow about 12 yards of woven cotton fabrics such as calicos or broadcloth, cut 1½ inches wide and double folded, or 8 yards of fabric if you are using unfolded strips one inch wide. When you are using odd yardages or old clothing allow yourself the equivalent of ½ yard for each wedge, so that you have a bit extra.

**Directions for 24-inch Round (or Half-Round) Wedge Knit Rug with a 4-Stitch Repeat:**

Use Size 15 (10 mm) knitting needles, 14 inches long, or circular.
Cast on 24 stitches
Row 1: Knit 4, turn work
Row 2: Slip 1, Knit 3, turn work

Row 3: Knit 8, turn work
Row 4: Slip 1, Knit 7, turn work

Row 5: Knit 12, Turn work
Row 6: Slip 1, Knit 11, turn work

Row 7: Knit 16, Turn work
Row 8: Slip 1, Knit 15, turn work

Row 9: Knit 20, turn work
Row 10: Slip 1, Knit 19, turn work

Row 11: Knit 24, turn work
Row 12: Slip 1, Knit 23, turn work

Rows 1 through 12 complete one 'wedge'. To make a full circle you will need to knit 24 wedges. To make each wedge a different color or shade, change colors at the end of row 12 on each repetition. Some fabrics will form a circle without knitting the full number of wedges. Lay the knitting down and if it forms a good circle at 21 or 22 wedges (without stretching), just skip the last two or three wedges. (To make a half-round rug, knit 12 wedges.)

**Lacing a Wedge Knitted Rug Together**

After you have completed the knitting, and cast off the stitches, lay the rug on a table. You will notice that there is a small open circle forming a "hole" at the center of the work. The first step in lacing is to pull this circle tight to form a firm center. (If you are making a half-round rug this center lacing is all that you will have to do. If you are making an oval, you will need to pull the center tight at both ends.) Lacing is done with the same fabric strip with which you knitted the rug. Cut a length of fabric strip 1½ to 2 times as long as the sections to be laced. Use a large-eye lacing or weaving needle.

**To lace the center:** Insert the lacing needle under all of the slip stitches at the very center of the circle. The needle should pass under only one loop of the fabric in each stitch. Pull the lacing tight, and anchor it with a few stitches with needle and thread. Make sure that the center is closed, but not pulled so tightly as to form a bulge.

**To lace the edges closed:** Once the center is laced, the edges of the first and last knitted wedges should lay nicely together. Begin at the center of the rug and use a whip stitch for lacing. Make sure as you lace that the outside corners match exactly. After the lacing is complete, work the lacing strip into the knitting and sew the end in place. Clip off any excess.

**To make a larger round center with the 4-stitch repeat:** In the knitting pattern, you will notice that the rows are all knitted in multiples of four stitches. You can make a larger wedge knitted rug by adding as many stitches as you can handle on your needles so long as the total number of stitches is a multiple of four.

**The general pattern for any wedge knit rug is:**

Cast on any number of stitches that is divisible by X. (X is the number of stitches in the repeat you have selected.)

Row 1: Knit X, turn work

Row 2: Slip 1, Knit X-1

**Odd numbered rows**: Knit X more stitches than in the last odd numbered row.

**Even numbered rows**: Slip the first stitch, then knit to end of row.

Repeat odd and even rows until all of the stitches on the needle are knitted in the even row. Then begin the next wedge by starting again at Row 1.

## *Enlarging Wedge Knitted Rugs with Rounds of Knitting*

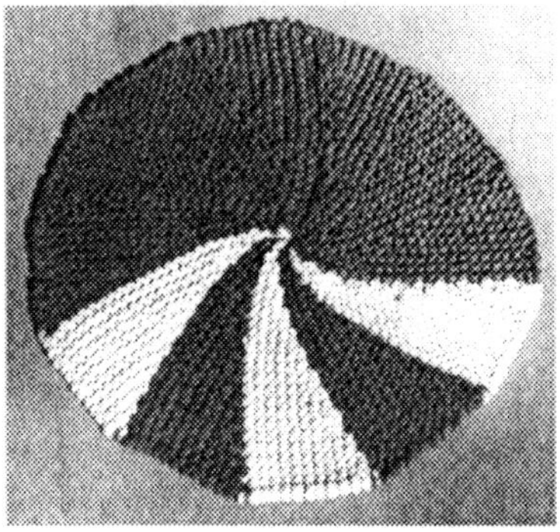

*Wedge knitted rugs can be made in asymetrical designs whre only a few of the wedges are in a contrasting color. The center of the rug shown here is a 24-inch cusing a four stitch repeat. Only three of the wedges are made with the light fabric.*

*With the addition of the first outer band (added bullseye-style), the design is beginning to show. Notice how the light colored sections draw the eye first.*

*Below is the completed rug with a second outer band added. The rug is about 48 inches across.*

**To make a larger rug by adding border strips**

Wedge rugs can be made larger by adding borders of knitting around the wedges. This is the same as the bullseye construction (see the next chapter).

**Using the stockinette stitch in a wedge knitted rug:**

The stockinette stitch can be used in the wedge knitted rug, but because it has different characteristics than the garter stitch, the edges of the rug will need to be finished off with a whip stitch, blanket stitch or crochet (see Handbook section). There is also a way to incorporate one line of garter stitching to accent each wedge, and overcome the tendency of the stockinette stitch to curl. The directions below are for both the plain stockinette and the accented stitch, since they are identical until row 10. The accenting forms raised lines of garter which radiate from the center of the wedge knit rug.

**Directions for 14 inch Round with Stockinette Stitch in 3-Stitch Repeat:**

Cast on 15 stitches
Row 1: Knit 3, turn work
Row 2: Slip 1, Purl 2, turn work

Row 3: Knit 6, turn work
Row 4: Slip 1, Purl 5, turn work

Row 5: Knit 9, turn work
Row 6: Slip 1, Purl 8, turn work

Row 7: Knit 12, turn work
Row 8: Slip 1, Purl 11, turn work

Row 9: Knit 15
Row 10: Slip 1, Knit 14 (for accented wedges) *or* Slip 1, Purl 14 (for plain stockinette)
Rows 1 through 10 make one wedge. Repeat these rows in sequence 18 times to make a full circle. (Repeat 9 times to make a half-circle.) See lacing instructions for the 16-inch round above.

## *Oval Wedge Knitted Rugs*

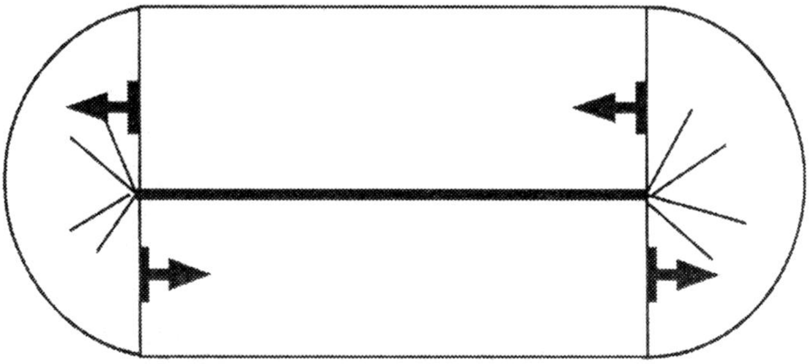

*Oval wedge knitted rugs area composed of two half-circles at the ends separated by secions of straight knitting. The oval is knitted in a single piece. Because only half of the width of the rug is knitted at a time, fairly large rugs can be made on 14-inch needles.*

*Below, a small oval is shown in progress. The wedges at one end, and one side of the straight knitting is complete. The wedges at the other end are just begun.*

## Oval Wedge Knitted Rugs

The process of knitting an oval rug with the wedge knit pattern is very simple—once you understand the basics of the wedge. To knit an oval, a section of straight garter stitching is added in the midsection of the rug. One half of the wedges are knitted at each end.

The dimensions of the finished rug are determined by the straight section of knitting. For example if you want a rug that is 2 feet wide and 4 feet long, your straight section of stitching must be two feet long (4 - 2 = 2).

These basic directions are designed to be used with the basic wedge pattern for 24-inch round rugs. You can increase the length of the rug by adding length to the straight knitted sections. You can add width to the rug by adding stitches (in multiples of four), or by adding more bands of knitting around the outside (see 'Bullseye' rugs).

**Directions for 24" X 36" Oval Wedge Knit Rug:**
Use size 15 (10 mm) needles, 14 inches long or circular
Cast on 24 stitches.
**Step 1:** First a straight section is knitted forming one side of the oval.
Slip 1, Knit 23 and repeat until knitting is 12 inches long
**Step 2:** Knit wedges at end
Follow the wedge pattern for 24-inch round rugs, completing 12 wedges.
**Step 3:** Knit straight side (Repeat Step 1)
**Step 4:** Knit wedges at end (Repeat Step 3)
**Lacing:** Follow the general lacing instructions for wedge knitted rugs. Oval rugs are laced together in the following order: centers of wedges; center of rug; then ends of knitted sections.

CHAPTER 8

# Bullseye Knitted Rugs

The bullseye pattern for knitting round rugs is made by combining a round wedge knitted center with narrow strips of garter stitching. The concentric rounds of knitting give the pattern its name. Since each section is knitted separately, the rug can be done as lap work. Large rugs are created by continuing to add knitted strips around the outside of the rug. Using the patterns any size round rug can be created. The same principles are used for oval rugs.

Fabric requirements are given for some of the rugs shown in this chapter, but you will doubtless want to make rugs that are larger or smaller or with different arrangements of fabrics. To estimate the fabric requirements for bullseye rugs, see the Handbook Section for the particular type of fabric you are using.

The center round can be knit in any size. Directions are for 8-inch and 16-inch round wedge knit centers are given in the previous chapter. The 8-inch center makes a round hotpad, and it is a good idea to make one just for the practice before beginning on the bullseye rug itself.

The width of the knitted bands around the center of a bullseye rug can be varied for particular effects. With an 8-inch center the first couple of bands should not be knit wider than eight stitches because these bands must be able to curve easily around the center. As a general rule, the first ring around the center of a bullseye rug should be made with the same or fewer stitches as were cast on for the round center. If you select the 16-inch center (made by casting on 16 stitches) the next round should have a maximum of 16 stitches as its width.

## *Round Bullseye Rug Basics*

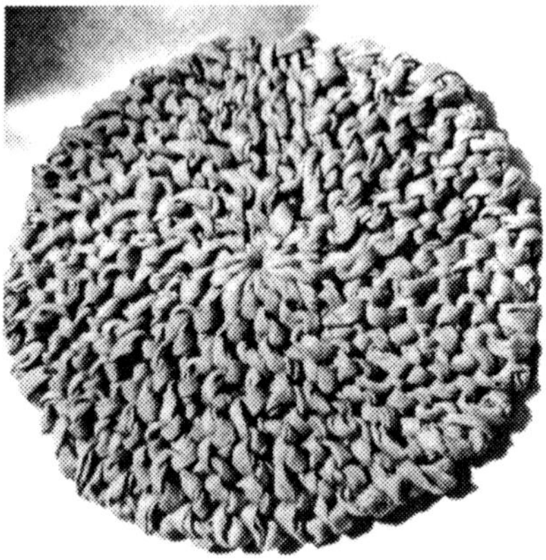

*Begin a bullseye rug with a round center section. The 8-inch center is shown at left.*

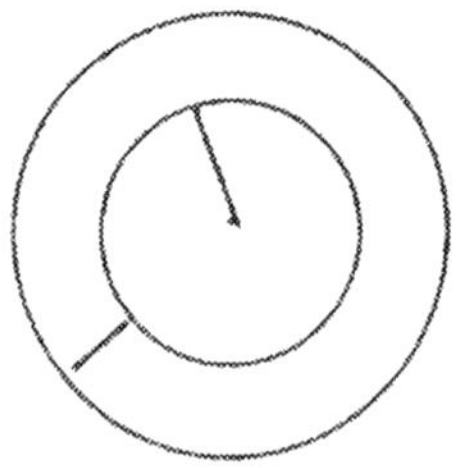

*Note that in the illustrations the seam line depicting the ends of a band are staggered around the rug. These ends should not line up or they can become prominent, since there is a slight variation in texture from the knitted portions.*

*Additonal rounds are added to the center to make the rug larger.*

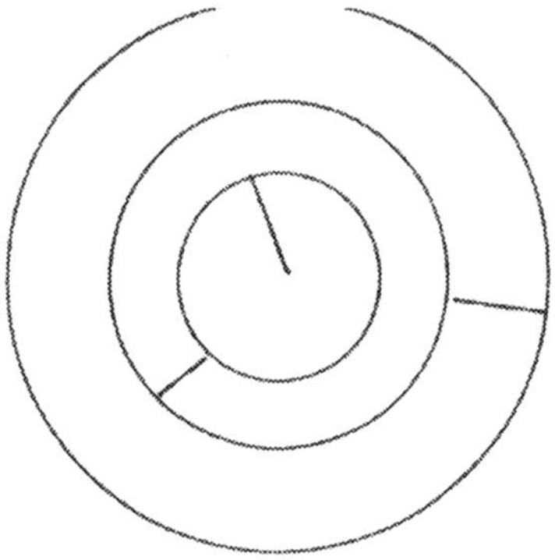

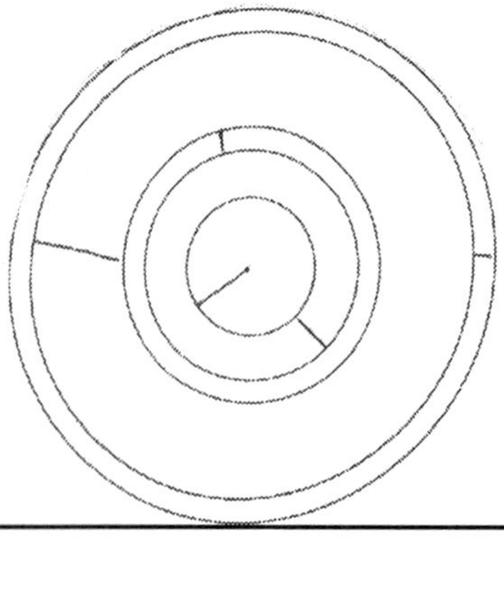

*Bullseye rugs are most interesting when the bands of knitting are of different widths. This is also a good way to accent colors or make a transition from one color to another, with a narrow band of an intermeditate tone in between.*

Any fabrics suitable for rugs can be used for the bullseye rugs. This technique has lots of design possibilities such as: gradations of colors; solid color rings combined with patterned rings; or a series of rings each with its own combination of colored blocks for a patchwork effect. There are some design considerations specific to bullseye rugs. Choose a medium tone for the center, not the darkest or lightest of the fabrics you plan to use. A very dark center will create a visual hole in the center, and a very light color will seem to pop out of the rug.

Even though this is named the bullseye pattern, unless you have a very modern decor, alternate rounds of light and dark are *not* recommended. The design is just too stark. For alternating rounds of two fabrics, make sure that they are close in tone and/or shade.

**General Directions for Round Bullseye Knitted Rugs**

Use size 15 (10 mm) needles for all fabrics.

**Step 1: Knit the Center Round:** Select one of the round center sizes in the previous chapter and complete it following the directions there.

**Step 2: Knitting the First Outer Band:** Whichever size rug center you choose, the outer bands of the bullseye rug are usually knitted in plain garter stitch. The directions below are for the 8-inch center, but you can modify the width of this band as you like if you have a larger center. If you chose the eight-inch round center, the first band cannot be wider than the 8 stitches given, but it can be narrower:

Cast on 8 stitches
Row 1: Slip 1, Knit 7
Repeat Row 1

If you used the 8-inch round center, your first band of knitting will need to be approximately 192 rows long.

**Step 3: Lacing the First Outer Band to the Center:** It is impossible to give exact lengths in rows since fabrics and knitting tightness will vary, so do not cast off until the band is laced almost all of the way around. Use a large-eye lacing needle or tapestry needle for the lacing. Thread the needle with the same fabric strip that was used in the knitting, and cut the fabric strip at least 1½ times the length of the section to be laced.

On a round rug you can begin lacing the outer band at any point except in line with the lacing of the center round. Of course you'll begin lacing the outer band with the cast on stitches. Lace the outer band to the rug center with a whip stitch, placing one stitch in each matching row. Keep the lacing snug, but don't pull it tight or it will buckle the rug. You do not need to knot the end of the lacing, instead just allow the last 6 inches or so of the fabric strip to remain loose. It will be laced back into the rug later.

Each row must be fitted around the rug. As you approach lacing the last few inches of the outer band, look to see if you need some additional length to make the band lay easily, and knit as many rows as may be needed to have the knitting fit exactly around the center. Then cast off the stitches. If the outer band looks too long to fit easily, unravel rows until it is the proper length and then cast off. Finish lacing the band to the center. Finally, lace the ends of the knitted band together.

Weave the ends of the lacing strip back into the knitting. Clip off any extra and sew the end in place so that it doesn't work loose in laundering. Do the same with the tag ends of strip where you cast on and cast off the stitches.

**To Continue: Knitting the Outer Bands:** Once the first outer band is completed, additional bands can be added in a wider range of knitted width. If you want all of the outer bands to be the same width, just cast on the same number of stitches. Or, each outer band can be of increasing width, or of variable widths. Whichever arrangement you choose, be sure to knit each band to fit exactly around the previous band, and don't cast off the final stitches until your lacing is nearly completed. These outer bands are laced to the rug just the same as the first outer band. Remember that each band must be knit to fit precisely around the previous band, so don't cast off until the lacing is nearly completed.

### Half-Round Bullseye Rugs

It is very easy to knit a half-round rug. Follow the directions for either the 8-inch or 16-inch center, but only knit six wedges. There are two ways to add the outer bands. The first results in a longish half circle (sometimes called a "Heelprint" rug). The other is a true half round as shown in the sketches. The only difference in constructing these two related shapes is the order in which the outer bands are added.

Whether you are knitting a true half-round or a heel-print, when you have knitted six wedges for the center, you will need to lace the center "hole" closed. Use a large-eye lacing needle. Thread it with the rug strip left from the original slip knot at the center of the half circle (where you cast on the stitches). Insert the needle into the opposite edge of the hole, and work it underneath each of the center stitches. Pull up on the strip to tighten up the hole, and then lace the strip into the knitting. Sew the end of the strip in place, and clip off any excess.

The photograph is of a sixteen inch half-circle. The same process is used for smaller or larger half-circles. Once the center half-round section is finished this way, it is time to begin knitting the outer bands.

**The "Sunset" Rug on the Cover: A Half-Round Bullseye Rug**

Of the various types of knitted rugs, the Bullseye rugs are often the most looked down upon because they are so simple to construct. I intentionally chose a half-round bullseye rug for the cover to show how striking these simple rugs can be.

The "Sunset" rug is made entirely of printed cotton fabrics. The 1½-inch strips were double-folded to hide the raw edges before knitting. The center is the sixteen-inch half circle (knit six wedges of the sixteen-inch center pattern). The fabric was a brilliant black, orange and white tropical print. (Notice how the print has disappeared in the knitting.) I allowed two yards of the 45-inch wide fabric for this section and had strip left over.

The half-circle was laced at its open center hole before the first band was added. The first band around the center was a dark tropical print with black, blue and purple predominating. It is knitted only 4 stitches wide with the garter stitch. (All of the rug is made with the garter stitch.) This band took just about ¾ of a yard of fabric.

The next band (the one with the radiating colors) was made from a *striped* fabric. It was chosen to show how easily you can get blocks of color into a knitted rug. Remember that the section was knitted with a straight garter stitch, the appearance of wedges only comes from the fact that the garter stitching was curved around the center. This band was knitted 12 stitches wide. The fabric was 7 yards long, so each "block" of color was a strip from the fabric 7 yards long. (Of course, there was a batch left over for other projects, since this band only took half of the strip.)

## *Half-round Bullseye Rugs*

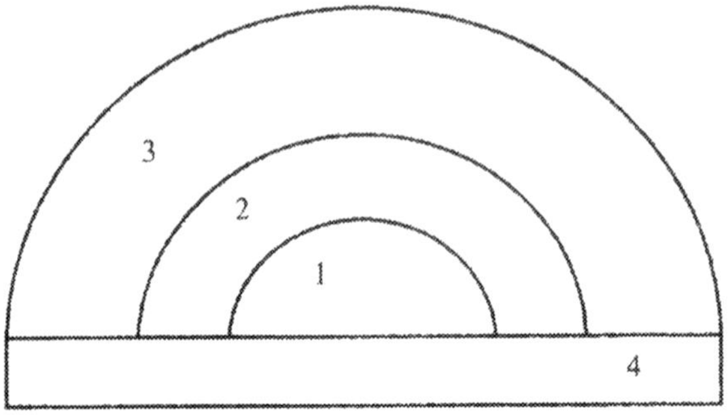


*Above is the assembly pattern for a true half-round bullseye rugs, and below is the heelprint pattern. Note that the numbers indicate the order in which the bands are added.*

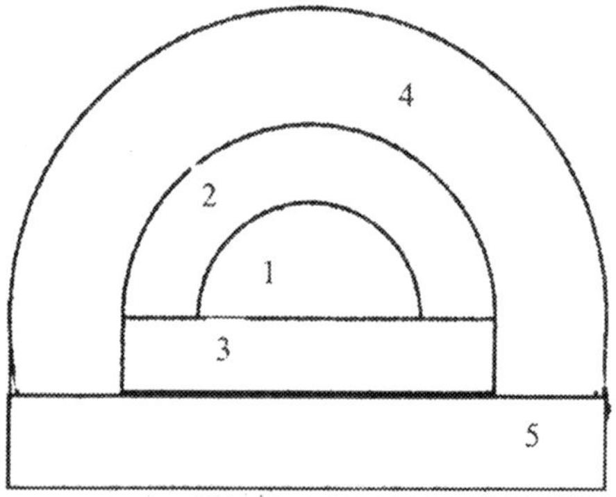

*A 16-inch half-round center for a bullseye rug shown just before lacing together the center "hole."*

The third and fourth bands were each knitted eight stitches wide. They were geometric prints in bold colors. The third band required just under five yards of fabric and the fourth band required about 6½ yards of fabric.

The base (straight section at the bottom) was knitted with the same geometric print as the third curved band. It is also eight stitches wide and required about 3½ yards of fabric.

Note that each and every band of knitting was fitted and laced to the rug before the next band was knitted. This lets each band be perfectly fitted.

**Oval Rugs in the Bullseye Style**

The bullseye construction can also be used to make an oval rug. The only difference is that the center is a long section of knitting, tapered and rounded at each end to allow the outer bands of knitting to curve around it.

**Center for an Oval Bullseye Rug, Eight Inches Wide.**

Before you begin an oval rug, you need to know what the finished size of the rug will be. The length minus the width of the finished rug will be how long the center knitting should be. For example if you want a finished rug 5 feet long and 3 feet wide, the center knitting will need to be 2 feet long (5 – 3 = 2).

**General Directions for Oval Centers:**

Use size 15 knitting needles (10mm), 14 inches long
Center section, eight inches wide in garter stitch. Knit to desired length.
Note that the stitches are always cast onto the working needle (right needle for right handers or left needle for left handers).
Cast on 8 stitches.
Slip 1, Knit 1, Cast on 1, Knit 6
Slip 1, Knit 1, Cast on 1, Knit 7
Slip 1, Knit 1, Cast on 1, Knit 8
Slip 1, Knit 1, Cast on 1, Knit 9
Slip 1, Knit 1, Cast on 1, Knit 10
Slip 1, Knit 1, Cast on 1, Knit 11
Slip 1, Knit 1, Cast on 1, Knit 12
Slip 1, Knit 1, Cast on 1, Knit 13
Slip 1, Knit 15

## *The Half-round "Sunset" Bullseye Rug*

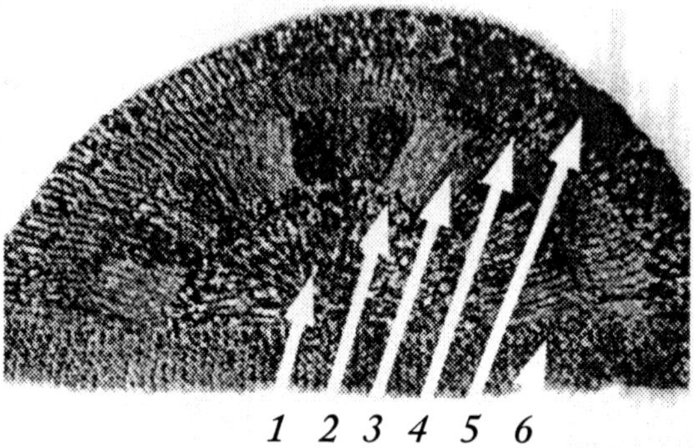


*The "Sunset" rug was knitted in six sections in the order shown by the numbers. See the text for fabric descriptions.*

*At right is a detail of section 3 which appears to have radiating bands of color.*

*Below is a photo showing the rug being assembled, with section 4 ready to be laced to the rug.*

You now have a total of 16 stitches on the needles.
Continue with a garter stitch (Slip 1, Knit 15) until this section measures about 3 inches shorter than the desired center length. Then begin decreasing the width of the knitted strip in the following way.

Slip 1, Knit 2 together, knit 13
Slip 1, Knit 2 together, knit 12
Slip 1, Knit 2 together, knit 11
Slip 1, Knit 2 together, knit 10
Slip 1, Knit 2 together, knit 19
Slip 1, Knit 2 together, knit 8
Slip 1, Knit 2 together, knit 7
Slip 1, Knit 2 together, knit 6
Cast off the 8 stitches remaining.

**Wider or Narrower Centers for Oval Rugs**

An eight-inch center is a good width for your first oval rug. It is wide enough to allow the outer bands to curve around easily and still not so wide as to dominate the rug. However, you may decide that a wider or narrower central band is just what your rug needs.

For a wider center band, begin as above by casting on eight stitches and follow along the pattern casting on one stitch in each row. Keep casting on until you reach the width that you want. Take note of how many rows of stitching it takes to reach the width and allow that same number to decrease to the curve at the other end. The tapering off curve is done by slipping one stitch, then knitting two stitches together at the beginning of each row. Cast off when there are eight stitches remaining on the needle. (Note that this procedure should not be done for oval centers wider than about 30 stitches. For wider centers, see the chapter on knitting rugs in one piece.)

For a narrower center band, begin by casting on half of the number of stitches you'll want in the band. For example, if you want your center band to be 10 stitches wide, cast on five stitches to begin. Increase the width at each row by casting on one in each row until you reach the desired 10 stitches. Likewise at the other end of the strip, decrease by knitting two stitches together in each row until only five stitches remain on the needle and then cast off.

## Outer Bands for Oval Bullseye Rugs

Outer bands for the oval rug are knitted just as for the round bullseye rug. The garter stitch is used and they can be of any width from 4 to 20 stitches (or wider for large rugs). The bands are eased around the curves at the ends and butted together. Each band is laced to the rug before the next band is knitted. The ends of the bands should be joined along one of the flat sides of the oval and alternate which side of the oval is used for subsequent knitted rounds that are added.

## The New England Style Alternative

Bullseye rugs in some parts of New England incorporate braiding with the knitting. Especially with oval bullseye rugs, this was a fairly common assembly. The center round (or oval) was knitted, then a 3-strand braid was laced or sewn to it. The ends of the braids were butted together. (Butting is the process of tapering the ends of the braided strips and interweaving them to disguise the joint. Since this is really a rug braiding method, I would refer you to a book on that subject if you have difficulty figuring it out.) Then the next band of knitting was added, then a round of braid and so on, ending with a braid at the outer edge.

This assembly style can be tricky in use, particularly since the braids were often made of woolen fabric while the knitted sections were of cotton fabrics. The braids, being thicker, stood up above the surface of the knitting and were subject to wear and catching the unwary walker. If you decide to try this style of assembly, the best option is to use light cottons or T-shirt single-knit fabric for both the knitting and the braiding. Cut the strips for braiding twice as wide as the ones for knitting.

## *Lacing the New England Alternative Bullseye Construction*

*This alternative construction places a round of bariding between rounds of knitting and the lacing technique is a little different than other bullseye rugs.*

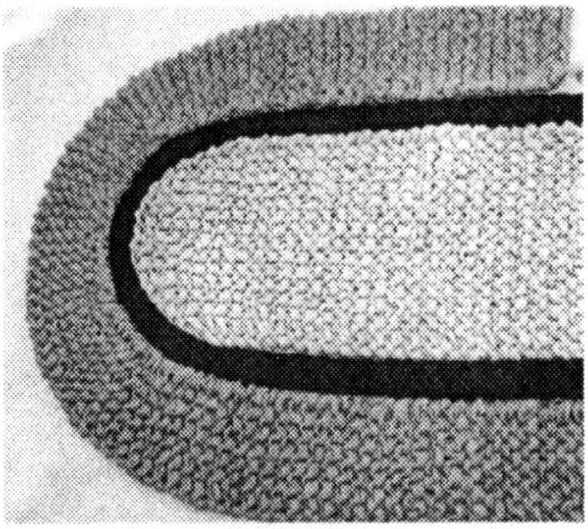

*Knit the center section of the rug and the next outer band, but do not cast off. Braid the insert so that it will fit around the center section and overlap about three inches. Do a test layout of the three pieces to make sure that they will lay easily without stretching and just touch each other all of the way around.*

*Secure the end of the braid with a safety pin or basting, and begin lacing about two inches from the braid end. Use the same strip for lacing as was used for the knitted portion. The lacing needle passses under a braid loop and then through a knitted row.*

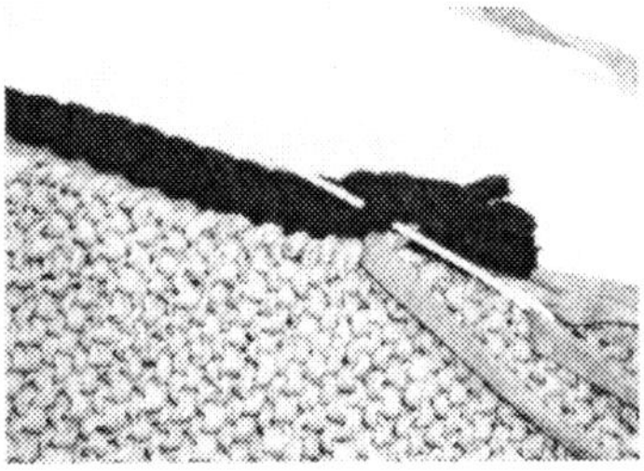

*Insert the needle under the very next braid loop, and pull the strip snugly to bring the braid and knitting together. Repeat where a row of knitting most closely lines up with the next braid loop.*

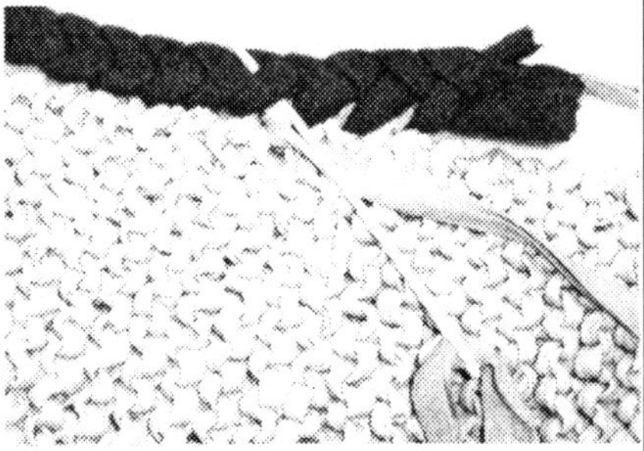

*The braiding and knitting will not line up precisely , but make sure that there is a lacing stitch through every one of the braid loops.*

CHAPTER 9

# *Winding Rugs*

The "winding" style of knitted rugs is a combination of the wedge and the strip construction. This style of rug is very striking and looks much more complicated than it is. In the photograph, each section is made with a different fabric, which accents the construction. The winding rugs are also particularly effective when made with a hit or miss selection of fabrics.

The width of the knitting in winding rugs can be as wide or narrow as you like. In the rug shown, the knitting is 12 stitches wide. These rugs can be made with strips of any even number of stitches. The straight portions are a simple garter stitch, knitted until the desired length is reached. The curved sections are knitted as wedges. The rows of knitting increase by two stitches with each repetition, just like the round centers for bullseye rugs.

The same technique as used for the winding path rug can be modified to frame a knitted rug. This is especially useful to round off sharp corners of a rug that may want to curl up. The frame itself can be quite decorative, and can be made as a narrow outline (four to six stitches wide) or as an outer band that substantially increases the size of the rug. At each corner of the rug, a quarter-circle is knitted which allows the band of straight knitting to turn 90 degrees.

**The "Winding Path" Rug**

To create the same effect as the rug in the photo, the fabrics needed are three different T-shirt cottons, 60 inches wide, 3 yards of

## *Winding Path Rugs*

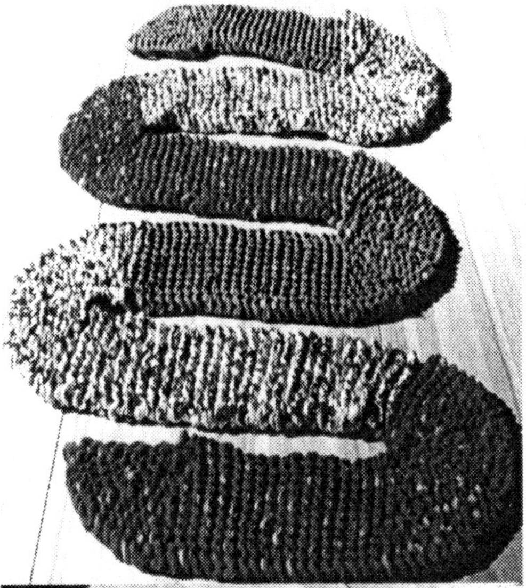

*The winding path rug is shown at left with the knitting completed.*

*Below is the rug with the lacing completed.*

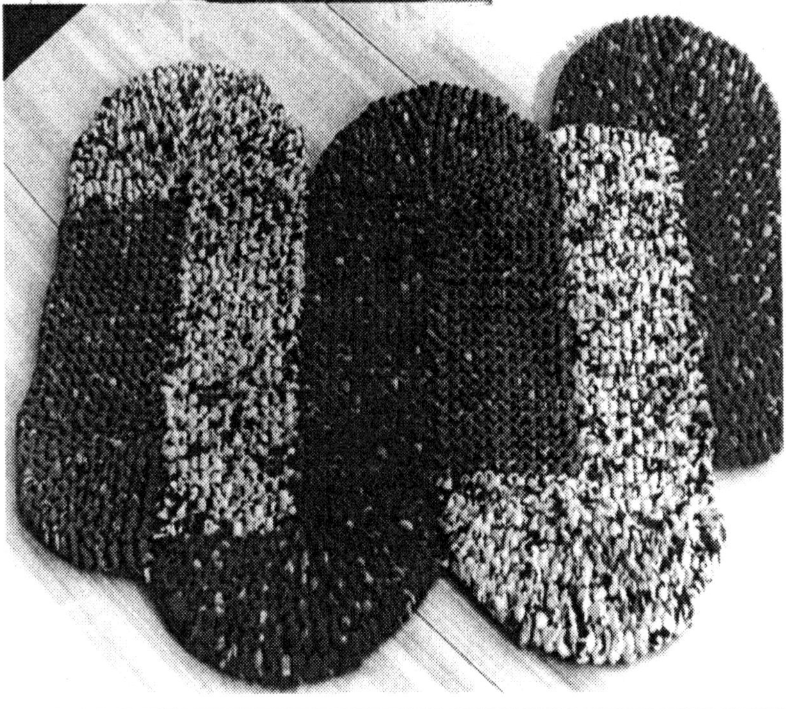

each, cut into 1 inch strips, *or* three different light cottons (calico, broadcloth, etc.) 45 inches wide, 4½ yards of each, cut into 1½-inch strips, joined and double-folded.

**Directions for Winding Path:**
Use size 15 (10mm) knitting needles.
Beginning with a quarter circle (equal to 3 wedges)
Cast on 12 stitches.
To knit one wedge:
Slip 1, Knit 1, turn work
Slip 1, Knit 1, turn work
Slip 1, Knit 3, turn work
Slip 1, Knit 3, turn work
Slip 1, Knit 5, turn work
Slip 1, Knit 5, turn work
Slip 1, Knit 7, turn work
Slip 1, Knit 7, turn work
Slip 1, Knit 9, turn work
Slip 1, Knit 9, turn work
Slip 1, Knit 11, turn work
Slip 1, Knit 11, turn work

Repeat the sequence until you have completed a total of three wedges.
This is a quarter-circle.
To knit straight section:
Slip 1, Knit 11
Repeat until 31 rows are complete.

**To knit first half circle:**
Knit 6 wedges.

**Change to second fabric.**
Knit a straight section of garter stitch 59 rows long.
Then knit a half circle (6 wedges)

**Change to third fabric.**
Knit a straight section of garter stitch 43 rows long.
Then knit a half circle (6 wedges)

**Change back to first fabric.**
Knit a straight section of garter stitch 47 rows long.
Then knit a half circle (6 wedges)

**Change to second fabric.**
Knit a straight section of garter stitch 55 rows long.
Then knit a half circle (6 wedges)

**Change to third fabric.**
Knit a straight section of garter stitch 37 rows long.
Then knit a quarter circle (3 wedges)

Note that the number of rows of straight garter stitching is always an odd number. That is so that each half circle will curve away from the previous knitting. If you are knitting a random length (or have lost count) just make sure that when you begin knitting a half or quarter circle, the first two stitches are on the outside edge of the curve. That way, even if you have miscounted the rows, the edge will still turn the right direction.

With a large eyed lacing needle, using a strip of any of the fabrics, lace the rug sections together. You can use a simple back-and-forth lacing or a whip stitch. Work on a flat surface when you do the lacing to make sure that the rug lies flat. When the rug is laced together, use the lacing needle to work the loose ends of the fabric strip into the rug. Stitch the ends in place and clip off any excess.

**Variations on the Winding Path**
You can make the winding path rug nearly to any size and configuration. The basic rules for the winding path construction are:
1. Begin and end with a quarter circle (3 wedges).
2. Alternate straight sections of garter stitch with half circles (6 wedges) through the rug.
3. If you want wider or narrower strips, just modify the wedge pattern to the appropriate (even) number of stitches.

CHAPTER 10

# *Hexagonal Block Knitted Rugs*

Hexagonal knitted rugs are a lot of fun to make. You can make just the hexagonal center and surround it with additional rounds of knitting, but the most fun is to make a rug that is entirely hexagonal blocks that are put together in the same fashion as hexagonal quilts. These are very striking and each hexagonal block makes a light piece of lap work.

Hexagons are made similarly to the wedge knitted round rugs using partial rows in a particular order. The directions which follow are for one hexagon that is 14 inches across (your dimensions may vary some, depending on the fabric you use).

For each hexagon allow 1½ yards of T-shirt knit fabric 60 inches wide, cut into 1-inch strips or 2¼ yards of light cotton fabric (calico, broadcloth, etc.) 45 inches wide, cut into 1½- inch strips, joined and double-folded. If you are going to make a bicolor hexagon, half of the required yardage should be of one color and the other half of the other color.

**Directions for 14 inch hexagon:**
Use size 15 (10 mm) knitting needles 14 inches long
Cast on 16 stitches.
The hexagon is composed of six sections.
To knit *one* section:
Slip 1, Knit 1, turn work.

Slip 1, Knit 1, turn work.
Slip 1, Knit 3, turn work.
Slip 1, Knit 3, turn work.

Slip 1, Knit 5, turn work.
Slip 1, Knit 5, turn work.
Slip 1, Knit 7, turn work.
Slip 1, Knit 7, turn work.

Slip 1, Knit 9, turn work.
Slip 1, Knit 9, turn work.
Slip 1, Knit 11, turn work.
Slip 1, Knit 11, turn work.

Slip 1, Knit 13, turn work.
Slip 1, Knit 13, turn work.
Slip 1, Knit 15, turn work.
Slip 1, Knit 15, turn work.
Slip 1, Knit 13, turn work.
Slip 1, Knit 13, turn work.
Slip 1, Knit 11, turn work.
Slip 1, Knit 11, turn work.

Slip 1, Knit 9, turn work.
Slip 1, Knit 9, turn work.
Slip 1, Knit 7, turn work.
Slip 1, Knit 7, turn work.

Slip 1, Knit 5, turn work.
Slip 1, Knit 5, turn work.
Slip 1, Knit 3, turn work.
Slip 1, Knit 3, turn work.

Slip 1, Knit 1, turn work.
Slip 1, Knit 1, turn work.

This completes one section of the hexagon. To make the complete hexagon, the directions above are repeated a total of six times. To alternate the colors in each section, change the color of the fabric strip that you are using as you begin each repeat. These directions look messy as the dickens, but it won't take long before you have them memorized and then the knitting goes quickly.

When the hexagon is finished, thread the lacing needle with the fabric strip, and begin lacing the hexagon together at the center. The center lacing should pull the "hole" shut. Then lace the two sides, using a back and forth or whip stitch. Work all loose ends of rug strip into the knitting and sew them in place. Clip off any excess.

**Bullseye assembly:** You can use your hexagon for the center of a simple bullseye style round rug. The outer rounds will need to be lightly gathered at the corners to accommodate the shape. This is a little trickier than working in the round. See the chapter on Bullseye rugs for finishing.

**All hexagon rug:** Make and finish as many hexagons as you like. Make sure to make half-hexagons for filling in if you want a (more or less) straight edge. A half-hexagon is made by knitting only three sections, and lacing closed the "hole" in the center similarly to the half-round bullseye center and half-round wedge shapes.

The hexagons are assembled into a rug by lacing them together with rug strip. Note that at each corner three different hexagons will touch each other. This is the only tricky bit in the assembly. You have to make sure that the three pieces join snugly at these corners and lay flat. Work on a flat surface when you do this final lacing.

Before you lace the rug together, lay out all of the hexagons to make sure that you like your design. Begin lacing at the center of the rug. (When doing this type of assembly, I lace the pieces with rug strip that is not longer than two feet. I leave both ends of the lacing strip free until all of the lacing is done and I have made sure that the rug is flat and all of the corners fit snugly. By doing this, I can readjust any lacing that isn't just right without having to hunt for its end.) When all of the lacing is completed. Work the loose ends into the knitting and stitch them in place. Clip off any excess.

## *Hexagonal Block Rugs*

*A completed hexagonal block rug, knitted in three colors, demonstrates the striking effects possible with the technique.*

*At left, a single hexagonal block, with the center "hole" laced closed and ready to lace into a rug.*

# CHAPTER 11

## *Heart Shaped Knitted Rugs*

*(and Other Special Shapes)*

Heart shaped rugs seem to be in fashion at the moment, and luckily heart shaped knitted rugs are pretty simple to make. There are two ways to knit heart shaped rugs. The easiest is made very much like an oval bullseye rug, except that there is a bend in the middle. The other alternative is to create a heart from a central square and two half-round wedge knitted section. Each of the knitted sections are "knit to fit" all based on the very first section that you make. Like most of the other types of knitted rugs, these look a lot more complicated than they are—so keep in mind that these are just plain garter stitches.

### A Modified Bullseye Heart Rug, 42 Inches Wide

Allow 9 yards of T-shirt knit fabric, 60 inches wide, cut into one-inch strips and joined together *or* 12½ yards of light cotton fabric (calico, broadcloth, etc.), 45 inches wide, cut into 1½ -inch strips, joined together and double-folded. To make the heart as shown in two colors, half of the material should be of each color.

### Directions

Use size 15 (10 mm) knitting needles, 14 inches long
The heart is made by piecing together four knitted sections.

## *Knitting a Heart Rug in Sections*

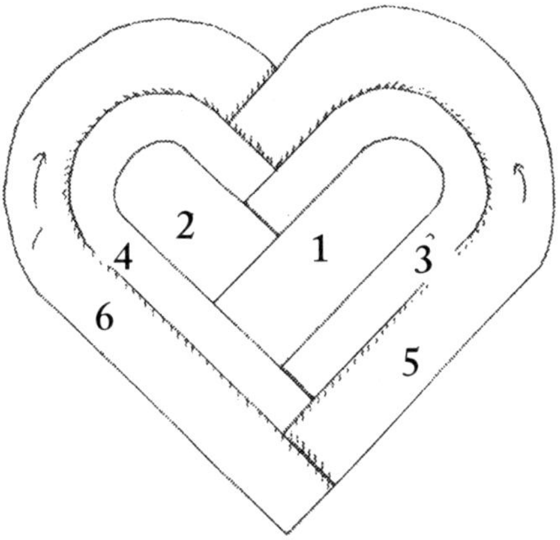


*At left is a diagram of how multiple sections can be joined to make a heart shape. Each section is numbered in the order it is knitted and joined to the rug.*

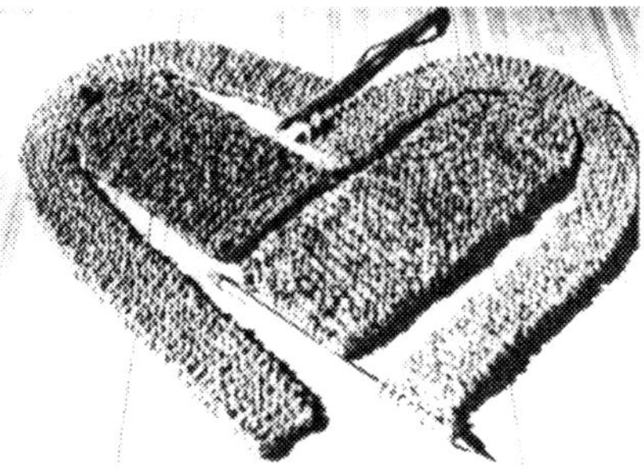

**First center section.**
Cast on 8 stitches.
Slip 1, Knit 7, Cast on 1
Slip 1, Knit 8, Cast on 1
Slip 1, Knit 9, Cast on 1
Slip 1, Knit 10, Cast on 1
Slip 1, Knit 11, Cast on 1
Slip 1, Knit 12, Cast on 1
Slip 1, Knit 13, Cast on 1
Slip 1, Knit 14, Cast on 1
Slip 1, Knit 15

You now have a total of 16 stitches on the needles. Continue with a garter stitch (Slip 1, Knit 15) until this section reaches 20 inches in length. Then cast off.

**Second center section.**
Repeat the directions for the first center section but stop knitting when the length of the second section plus the width of the first section add up to 20 inches (or the exact length of the first knitted section if it isn't 20 inches long). Place the two center sections at right angles to each other as shown and lace them together.

**Outer rounds**
All of the rest of the rug is knitted (in a plain garter stitch) to fit exactly around the two center sections. For **section #3**, cast on 8 stitches and knit it to length (see sketch). This section is then laced to the heart center, beginning at the 'point' of the heart. Lay the heart center on a table and begin lacing section #3 to the rug, easing the outer strip around the curve. I don't usually cast off until the lacing is nearly completed, which lets me add a row or two of knitting if needed before casting off.

Knit **section #4** for the other side of the heart just the same (8 stitches wide with plain garter stitch) until it fits around the curve of the heart. Then lace it to the center of the heart as shown in the sketch. When section #4 is laced to the rug, you can consider the heart completed, but if you want to increase the size of the rug, two more sections can be added as in the sketch, creating a heart that is almost five feet across. For **sections #5 and #6,** cast on 12 stitches and then lace them to the rug as each is completed.

**For larger hearts with the 'bullseye' method**

The basic process of knitting a heart rug is the same no matter what size rug you want. You can make larger hearts by increasing the length of the very first center section. For each six inches longer that you make the first section, the finished rug will be about a foot wider. (Of course with larger rugs you'll also need to add more rounds of the straight knitting to keep the proportions.)

Outer rounds are all knitted in a simple garter stitch and laced in the order shown in the sketch. The width of the strips going around the outside of the heart can be as narrow as four stitches wide or up to 16 stitches wide. Note that the outer rounds of the heart are knit and assembled in corresponding pairs. Both paired sections must be the same number of stitches wide.

A delightful "country look" heart rug can be made by mixing in a lot of colors in the very last pair of outer bands. This gives the effect of blocks of color around the heart for a real folk art effect.

Once you understand the principle of the heart rug assembly, it is really easy to make unique shapes of rugs using the same idea. For example, you can use four centers to make a lucky four-leaf clover rug.

**A Modified Wedge Knit to Form a Heart Shape**

The second way to make a heart is to think of the heart shape as a combination of two half rounds set on a square. (See the illustration on the next page.) You can use any of the half round centers in the chapter on wedge knitting. Knit two of these half rounds. Close up the center "hole" with lacing on each of the half rounds. Then knit a square, which is actually done by casting on twice as many stitches as you used for the center.

For example, if you used the 16-stitch half round, knit one square section that is 32 stitches wide. Knit as many rows as necessary to have your square exactly fit the base of the half rounds. (If you can't get 32 stitches on your knitting needles, instead knit two strips 16 inches wide and join them together.)

## *Knitting a Heart Shaped Rug in Three Pieces*

*Heart shaped rugs can be knitted in just three pieces: two half-rounds set on a central square. Above is the rug shown in progress with the half-rounds completed and the square just begun.*

*Below is the completed rug with the three sections laced together.*

CHAPTER 12

# *Rake and Spool Knitting plus "Idiot Cord" Rugs*

Rake and spool knitting are novelty methods of making knitted rugs. As the name implies, "rake knitting" is done on the tines of a rake or you can make your own "rake" with some nails or pegs in a stout board. Rake knitting is one of the easiest and possibly the oldest form of knitting. Making a rake knitted rag rug can be a project for children, or for the whole family with each member taking a hand. However, note that rake knitting is generally slower than using needles.

For rug construction, the most practical type of rake knitting is the double-sided, solid knitted type. It is a way to get a large rug knitted in one piece, which comes off the frame ready to use. If you have trouble with your hands, this is the technique to use to get a large rug.

While the term "Rake Knitting" may be unfamiliar, chances are that you are already familiar with the related technique. As a child you probably did "spool knitting" with yarn on the inside of an old wooden spool of thread. "Spool Knitting" used with fabric strip is the same process on a larger scale. "Idiot Cord" rugs create the same round strand of knitting as results from spool knitting, but "Idiot Cord" rugs are done with knitting needles and are much more quickly made.

## *Real Rake Knitting*

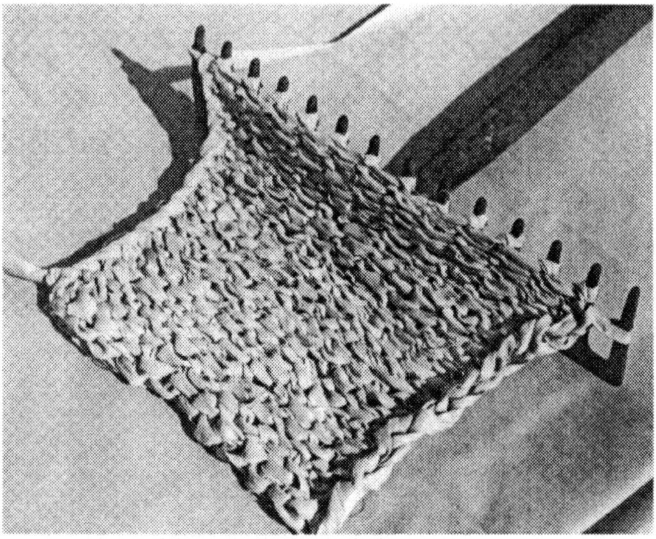

*Two views of a rug knitted on the tines of an old rake. Notice that the knitting is in the stockinette pattern because all of the loops were lifted from the handle side of the rake. For a garter stitch with the same procedure, alternate rows would have been worked from the other side of the tines. The knitting pulls up and is narrower than the rake itself because the fabric used was a one-inch cotton strip. Wider strips and heavier fabrics will show less decrease in width.*

**To Make Your Own Rake for Knitting Rugs (Single Layer)**

These rugs are particularly fun with children if you use a real garden rake. If you don't want to use a real rake (or if yours has seen too many leaves or whatever) you can make a stand to do rake knitting. Use at least a piece of 1" x 4" finished lumber, cut a little bit longer than you want for the width of the knitting. Mark a straight in the approximate center of the board, running lengthwise. Along this line firmly nail 8d (eight penny) or 10d (ten penny) finishing nails. My preference is to use drywall screws since they hold solidly, but the holes must be predrilled so you don't split the board. For a nicer looking rake you can use wooden dowels or craft pegs. Space the nails, pegs or screws evenly. If you are using fabric strip that is of medium to light weight, space the nails ½ -inch apart on center. If you are using heavy fabric strip space the nails ¾- inch apart on center. Make sure that the nails or screws are firmly set, but do not come through to the back of the board. The tines of your 'rake' should stick up above the board ½ to one inch. See the note below if you are making a rake large enough to knit a rug in single piece.

**Making a Rake Knitted Rug on a Single Set of Tines**

If you are going to use a real garden rake, the rug is just like the basic strip knitted rugs. Several narrow strips of rake knitting are assembled to form larger rugs just as if they were knitted on needles. You can use any fabric strip prepared as for knitted rugs but the easiest fabrics to handle are light cottons cut or torn about one inch wide. Really thick rugs done with a rake method are best made with wool strip cut ½ to ¾ inches wide.

**Step 1. Wrap the tines or pegs.** Make a slip knot in the end of the rag strip. Set the loop over a peg at the left end of the rake. Wrap the strip around each tine (or nail) in turn until you reach the end of the row. Position the loops so that they don't slip off of the tines.

**Step 2. The first row of rake knitting.** You may have seen spool knitting with yarns where two loops of yarn are around a peg, then the lower loop is lifted over the top loop. This procedure is a real struggle when using fabric strip since it just doesn't stretch. Instead a crochet hook (size J to L) is used as follows. With the hook, lift the loop of strip *all of the way off* the first tine. Then pull a loop of strip through the loop on the hook (a crochet chain stitch), and replace this new loop back onto the tine. Repeat the same process with each tine until you reach the other end of the rake.

**Step 3. The second row of rake knitting.** When the first row is complete, you will repeat the same process going back the other direction across the rake. Note that the end pegs will have only one stitch on them and as you reverse directions, the initial stitch in the next row is done on the second tine from the end.

If you always keep the fabric strip to the same side of the rake in each row, the rug will be in a stockinette stitch. If you alternate sides with each row across, the rug will be in a garter stitch. For the second row (and all future rows) skip the first tine and begin with loop on the second tine. Continue across the row pulling a loop off with the crochet hook, pulling a loop of strip through the loop on the hook, and putting the new loop back onto the tine of the rake.

**Step 4. Complete the knitting.** Repeat the second row directions until your knitted strip reaches the length you desire, then cast off using the crochet hook. Pull the loop off the first tine *at the opposite end of the rake* from where the fabric strip attaches. Then pull the loop off the second tine so that you have two loops on the crochet hook. Pull the "second" loop through the "first" loop, so that only one loop remains on the hook. Continue across the rake until all of the loops have been removed from the tines of the rake. When you reach the end of the rake, pull the end of the fabric strip up through the final loop.

**A few things you should note about single tine rake knitting.** You may find that the knitting will "pull up" as it progresses and become narrower than the rake, sometimes by as much as one-third. This narrowing is usually because the tines of the rake are a little more widely spaced than will exactly match the weight of the fabric you are knitting. This narrowing can be minimized by using wider strip or spacing the tines of the rake a little more closely. If you've gotten ambitious and want to make a rake knitted rug in one piece, do a test sample with your fabric strip to check for how much the knitting will pull up and adjust the width of your strips if the knitting wants to pull up too much.

**Double Sided Rake Knitting**

This is a variation that allows a heavy, more durable rug to be knit on a frame. The rake is made on a board as the base and is fairly simple to build. For the sides you will need two finished boards of 1-inch lumber (which is actually ¾" thick if you measure it). The boards can be 1" X 2" to 1" X 4" widths. Cut the boards to the desired rug width plus an allowance to accommodate the end bracing. If you look at the photograph of the frame, you'll see the end braces will take up room on the frame. For the end braces, also use 1" boards cut to length to allow them to span the side boards with a ¾" gap between them. Sand all of the boards so that they are smooth before you assemble the frame. Then nail or screw the side boards on top of the end boards as shown in the photograph. There should be an even ¾" gap between the side boards and the frame should be squared up.

**Setting the tines.** Usually for this type of rake knitting ¼-inch diameter wooden dowels are preferred since they make the nicest looking frame. (In the frame shown in the photograph, I used 1" drywall screws instead since they are very easy to work with.) The pegs should be spaced about an inch apart along each side, but the pegs should not line up across the gap between the side boards. Place the first dowel even with the end of the slot, and set all of the dowels on that side. Then set the dowels on the other side so that they are offset from the first line of dowels. The dowels should not line up on the two sides of the slot. There should be an odd number of total dowels. The dowels, pegs, screws or nails should stick up above the board ½ to one inch.

If the tines are properly set, there will be one more peg on one side of the slot than the other and that row of pegs will be longer. The shorter row of pegs on the opposite side will be inset at both ends when compared to the longer row.

**Making a Hollow Rug.** Have your fabric strip all prepared and rolled into balls. For a hollow rug, the fabric strip is wound in sequence around each peg in order. Begin at the last peg of the shorter row of pegs. If you are right handed, wrap the pegs in a counterclockwise direction (left handed: wrap clockwise). A slip knot holds the fabric strip on the first peg. (See the photograph.) Mark this peg with a permanent marker so that you know when you have completed a round. Twist the fabric strip around each peg one time.

## *Building a Double-Sided Rake*

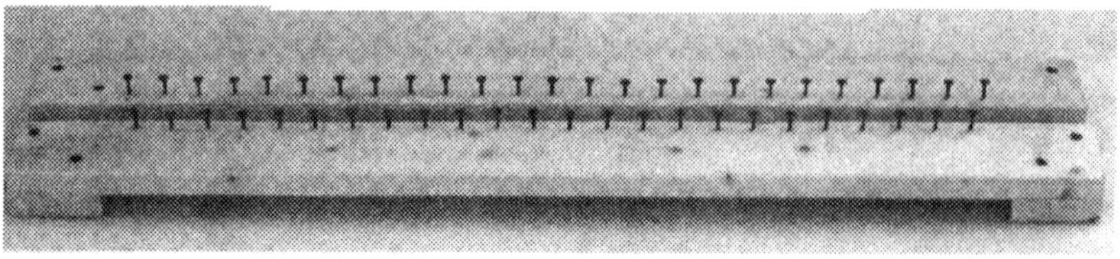

*Using one-inch lumber, cut the side pieces the width of the desired rug plus allowing for the end braces of the same lumber. Sand all of the pieces smooth. Use screws or nails to secure the side pieces to the end braces so that there is a 3/4-inch gap between the two side rails. Dowels, screws or nails are placed along the sides one inch apart and half an inch from the edge. These pegs are offset in the two rows across the gap. There should be an odd number of total pegs, and the row of pegs on one side of the frame will be longer than the other. The end pegs in the long row are called "turning pegs."*

*Wrapping the frame for a hollow rug*

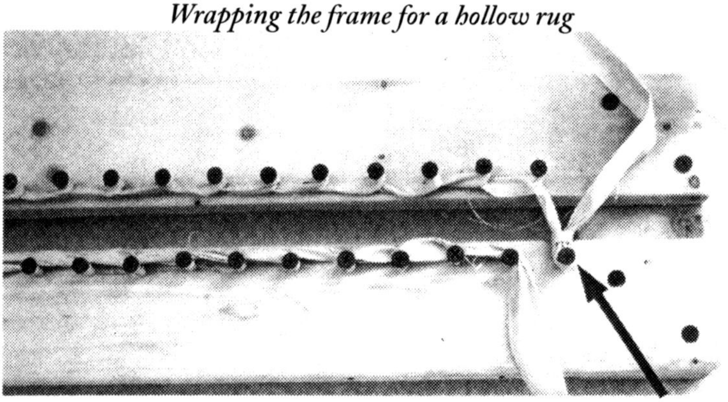

*Make a slip knot in the rug strip and slip it over the end peg in the long row. Then twist a loop in the strip over the end peg on the other side of the gap. Twist a loop around each peg in sequence going all of the way around the frame until you reach the beginning point. Start knitting with the peg with the slip knot.*

Hold the end of the strip to the inside of the two rows of pegs to get a stockinette stitch on both sides of the rug. Then the knitting proceeds just as for the single layer rake knitting, working each peg in sequence around the slot going the same direction (clockwise or counterclockwise). Use a crochet hook (size J to L) to pull the loop completely off of the peg, chain one stitch and then place the new loop onto the peg. Note that you can create a stockinette stitch if you always work with the strip to the inside of the pegs and a garter stitch if you make alternate rounds with the strip held to the outside (away from the slot).

Casting off is just the same as the single layer rake knitting also. The rug created is a hollow tube so the ends will need to be laced or crocheted closed. There really isn't any advantage to making a hollow rug unless you plan to insert a pillow or padding to make it softer for lounging on the floor. If you want a rug to be used for walking on, use the solid construction instead.

**Making a solid rug.** Construct a frame for double-sided rake knitting as described above. You can use T-shirt knit fabric cut 1 inch wide or light cotton fabrics cut or torn 1 inch wide. The nicest looking and most durable of these types of rugs are made with light cotton fabrics cut 1½ inches wide and double-folded allowing. Allow about 2 yards of fabric for each square foot of rug if you are using new fabric. Have your fabric strip all prepared and rolled into balls.

Make a slip knot in the fabric strip and put the loop over the first dowel at the end of the rug. Then move across to the opposite side of the slot and twist a loop over the first dowel there. Come back to the first side and twist a loop over the second dowel, then across to the second dowel on the opposite side. Then the third dowel and so on until you reach the opposite end.

Then you'll begin the actual knitting, but it will be worked on alternate sides of the frame just as the initial wrapping, and following the same path. As you work, always keep the fabric strip over the center gap between the two rows of pegs. Begin at the last peg wrapped, and using a size J to L crochet hook, pull the existing loop completely off the peg and onto the hook. Then pull a loop of strip through the loop on the hook and put the new loop back on the peg. Repeat the process with the first loop on the other side of the gap. Then following the wrapping, work back and forth until you reach the other end of the rake. Try very hard not to twist the new loops as you are working, or you will get a different texture than you were planning.

When you get to the further end where the original slip knot is, make a new loop for it and then just start back again. The end pegs in the longer row are called the "turning pegs" since they form the end of the row and only have one loop worked over them as you change directions. Most people find that turning the frame with each row is the easiest way to keep a consistent product. Also, don't feel that you have to work tightly. The rug will find its own tension with the fabric strip.

After you have made two or three rows of rake knitting, the rug will be forming in the gap between the two boards. Give a little tug on it to keep it headed in the right direction every couple of rows.

When the rug is as long as you want, cast off with the crochet hook beginning with the peg that is farthest from the end of the fabric strip. Pull off the loop. Then move across to the opposite peg and pull the loop off of it (two loops will be on the hook). Pull the second loop through the first loop so that there is only one loop on the hook. Continue to the next peg and repeat the process. The order of pulling off the loops goes back and forth across the slot just as the knitting did.

**Making a Solid Rug with Different Textures.** In the directions above, you're instructed to always keep the fabric strip to the center and make sure that the loops aren't twisted. That procedure is the easiest to follow and results in a rug with a ribbed stockinette texture on both faces of the rug. If you were to reproduce this texture on needles, it would be a knit 1, purl 1 pattern across the rug.

Handling the strip differently will give you different textures in the rug. For a knitted rug without the ribbing, the strip is held to the inside of one peg and the outside of the next. That will result in a stockinette stitch rug with two different face textures. Of course, if you feel really creative, you can alternate rows, or several stitches within a row to create your own pattern. Be warned though that too many variations in one rug will make it look like you made a mistake in the rug, so plan carefully.

If you twist the loops around the pegs each time, and reverse the direction of the twists in each row, you'll end up with a zig-zag

*Beginning a Solid Rug on a Double-sided Rake*

*Make a slip knot in the fabric strip and place it on an end peg in the long row. Then twist a loop over the first peg on the opposite side. Continue working back and forth until all of the pegs are wrapped.*

*At the opposite end of the frame, the last peg wrapped should be on the same side as the slip knot at the beginning.*

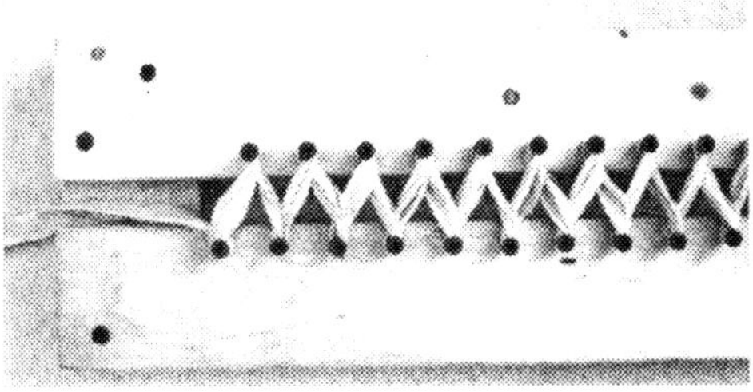

*Insert a crochet hook into the loop that was twisted over the last peg. With the hook, lift the loop completely off of the peg.*

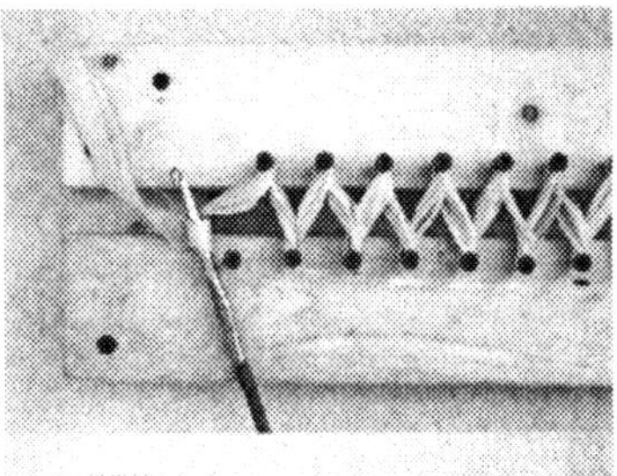

*Pull a loop of fabric strip through the loop on the hook. This is exactly like a chain stitch in crochet. Using the hook, place the loop back on the peg.*

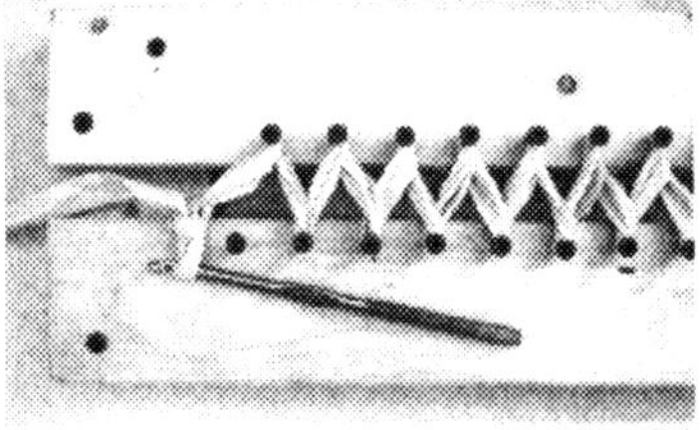

*Insert the hook in the first loop on the opposite side of the gap, and lift the loop off of the peg. Make a chain stitch and place the loop back on the peg. Continue with the same process working back and forth across the gap.*

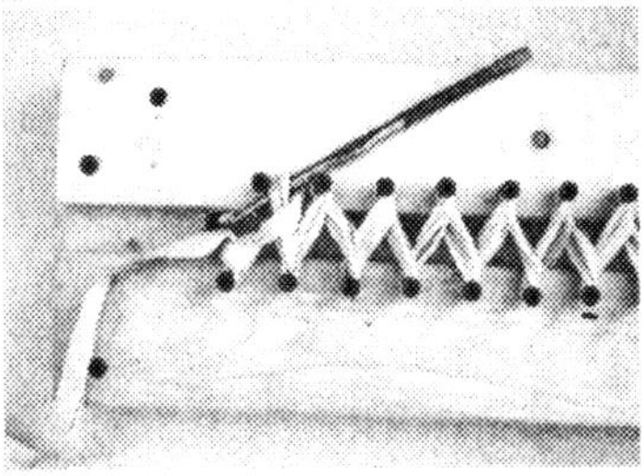

sort of texture which can be interesting. You can use that procedure if you really want to disguise how the rug was made.

**Making a Lighter Weight Solid Rug.** This variation produces a solid rug but it is not quite as thick as the regular procedure above. This type of rug does make up more quickly though. Wrap the tines as for the regular solid rug. The knitting goes back and forth across the gap also, but the knitting itself is slightly different. With the crochet hook, pull off a loop from the peg. Pull through a loop of strip (one chain stitch) and then pull through a second loop for another chain stitch. Put the second chain stitch back onto the peg. Finishing off is just the same as the rug above.

**Spool Knitting**

Spool knitting is just rake knitting done in the round and on a smaller scale. Recently the craft stores have featured a plastic spool supposedly for making rag rugs but it isn't really practical since the spool has four pegs and makes a braid which is too thick for a practical rag rug. It is easy enough to make your own spool for rug making with a small piece of wood. Choose a 1" X 4" board, cut 3 to 4 inches long, or a similar material. Drill a one-inch hole in the center of the board and sand all of the edges smooth. Place *three* dowels (or nails or drywall screws) evenly around the outside of the hole and about ¼ to ½ inch from the edge.

Use light cotton fabrics cut or torn one inch wide. These should be sewn into a continuous length using the overlapping bias joint and rolled up into a ball. Make a slip knot in the end of the fabric strip and set it over one peg. Twist a loop in the strip and slide it over the second peg and do the same with the third peg. That will bring you back to the start.

Use a J to L crochet hook to *remove* the slip knot completely from the first peg, and onto the hook. Put the fabric strip over the hook and pull up a loop (this is the same as a crochet chain stitch). Slip the new loop back onto the first peg. Move to the second peg and repeat the process, pulling the loop off, chaining one and setting the new loop back on the peg. Continue with the third peg and around and around continuously. A long 'rope' of knitting will be formed coming out the bottom of the hole in the board.

When you have several feet of knitting completed, you can begin coiling your rug. Round or oval shapes work best. The rounds of knitting are laced to the rug with the same strip as was used for the knitting, using a large-eye lacing needle, tapestry needle or any other blunt tipped needle that is large enough to handle the strip. Work on a flat surface as you are lacing and do not stretch the knitting around the rug. That will cause it to cup. Instead the knitted rope should lay gently touching the edge of the rug as you lace. Work back and forth with fairly small weaving and pull the lacing snug every few stitches. When you hold the rug up to the light you should not see light between the rounds of the knitting (lacing too loose) nor should the rug pucker (lacing too tight).

If your rug begins to cup, it means that you are pulling too much on the outside braid as you lace it to the rug (or you are pulling the lacing too tight). If your rug begins to form waves, the outside braid has too much slack as it is being laced to the rug. These knitted cords are quite forgiving though, and a little unevenness in the lacing will flatten out when the rug is in use.

You can alternate knitting with rug assembly until your rug is as large as you like. When your rug reaches the size that you want, you will need to taper the width of the rope so that it lays smoothly at the edge of the rug. If you are making an oval shape, plan to have the knitting end around a curved end, not along a straight side.

With the crochet hook, pull the loop off the next *two* pegs, crochet *one* chain through both loops and put it back on one of the pegs. You now have two pegs with loops on them. Work back and forth between them with the usual procedure four or five times. Then with the crochet hook, pull the loops off both remaining pegs. Chain one stitch through both loops. Then make four or five chain stitches with the hook and pull the end of the strip up through the last chain. Lace the last of the knitted strip to the rug including those final chain stitches. Then lace the end of the fabric strip back into the rug and sew it in place so that it doesn't work loose in laundering.

### Spool Knitting, A Quicker Variation

This variation makes a slightly more "open" rope with spool knitting, but goes faster. The resulting rug will also have a lower profile

## *Spool Knitted Rugs and "Idiot Cord"*

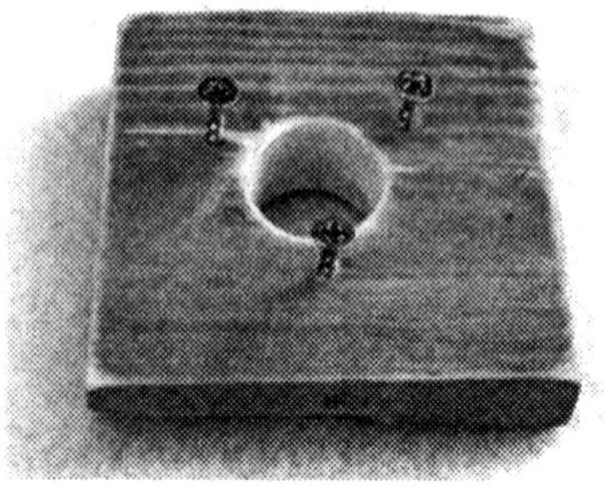

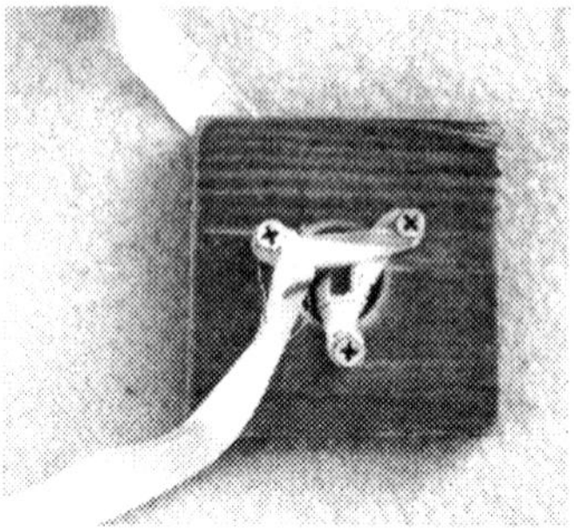

*A spool for knitting is easily made with a piece of scrap lumber and 3 drywall screws. See the text writtin driections for wrapping.*

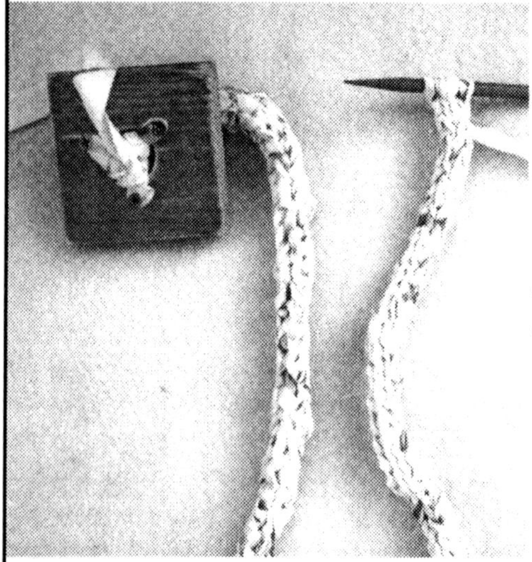

*At the left is a side-by-side comparison of a spool knitted rope and some "idiot cord" knitted with the same fabric. You can knit idiot cord about twice as fast as using the spool. See the text for directions.*

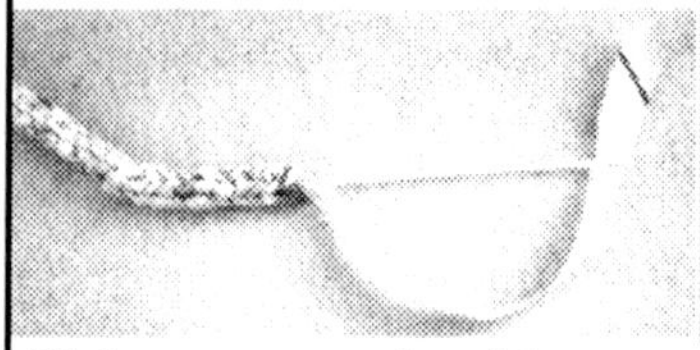

*To lace a rug made with either method, begin by lacing the fabric strip tail into the braid. Then with a new piece of strip lace back and forth in each stitch for a strong rug.*

because the knitted braid lays flatter, so if you want to make a rug that isn't quite as thick, use this method. Make your spool for the knitting exactly the same way as for regular spool knitting. Use light cotton fabrics cut one inch wide. These should be sewn into a continuous length using the overlapping bias joint and rolled up into a ball.

Make a slip knot in the end of the fabric strip and set it over one peg. Twist a loop in the strip and slide it over the second peg and do the same with the third peg. That will bring you back to the start.

Use a crochet hook to remove the slip knot from the first peg. Put the fabric strip over the hook and pull up a loop. Then chain one stitch through that loop. Slip the new loop back onto the first peg. Move to the second peg and repeat the process, pulling the loop off, chaining two stitches and setting the last loop back on the peg. Continue with the third peg and around and around continuously.

This variation is assembled and ended just the same as for regular spool knitting. See the directions above.

**"Idiot Cord" Rugs Made with Knitting Needles**

I learned this yarn technique at my grandmother's knee and she always referred to it as "idiot cord." I've seen some references to the same technique since and the writer always called it "idiot"-something (idiot knitting, idiot's delight, etc.) so I have to bow to tradition and also call it "idiot cord" even though it is quite an efficient way of making an attractive rug.

This method makes a round knitted cord—virtually identical to spool knitting—and you can make an "idiot cord" rug in about *half the time* as spool knitting. The cord is coiled and laced together just like a spool knitted rug. The technique uses double-ended knitting needles or circular needles. Try for size 15 needles, but if you can't find them, you can use a slightly smaller size, or make your own double-ended needles out of a half-inch wooden dowel, cut into 6-inch lengths, sharpening both ends and sanding smooth. One-inch strip of woven cottons work well, or you can use T-shirt knit fabric also an inch wide.

**Directions for "Idiot Cord" rugs:**
Cast on 3 stitches, turn work
Knit 3 stitches, do not turn work. Instead, slide the stitches to the other end of the needle.
Bring the strip around behind the needles to the working end and knit 3.
Again, slide the stitches to the other end of the needle, bring the strip around and knit 3 (repeat until knitted cord reaches several feet in length).

As you bring the strip around, try to keep some tension on it, but it doesn't have to be super-tight. This technique produces the knitted "rope" about twice as fast as with spool knitting. When you have several feet knitted, you can begin lacing the rope into the rug shape that you want. See the spool knitting directions above for the lacing. Then alternately knit more idiot cord and lace it to the rug. Change colors occasionally to create bands of different colors in the rug if you like.

When the rug is the size that you want, begin tapering the idiot cord by knitting two stitches together. There will be two stitches left on the needles. Continue to make more idiot cord using the two stitches for about six inches. Then knit those two stitches together. Remove the last stitch from the needles, and insert crochet hook about size L to N. Chain several stitches until there is about three or four inches of chain. Then pull the strip up through the last chain and clip it off, leaving about a 6-inch tail to lace back into the rug. Then finish lacing the cord to the rug. When it is all laced, work the tails back into the rug and secure the end with a few hand sewn stitches. Clip off any excess. If you are making an oval rug, plan to do the tapering and ending along one of the curved ends so that it will show less.

# CHAPTER 13

# *Woven and Cross-woven Knitted Rugs*

There are several methods to combine the techniques of weaving with knitting. These rugs will generally have more body and a lower profile on the floor than other knitted rugs since the weaving itself imparts those characteristics. The only real limitation in these rug techniques is that the knitting is not flexible and so the rugs have to be handled as strip rugs or knitted in a single piece.

The simplest way to obtain the effect of weaving in knitted rugs is to use the "fabric stitch" (also called the "woven stitch") as you knit the rug. The woven or fabric stitch results in a tight, even surface. The "woven" texture on the front side creates interest while the reverse texture is pebbly, resembling a Berber carpet. This technique has the advantage of using only a single strip of fabric at a time and is done in only one step, unlike the other rugs in this chapter which all use two (or more) fabric strips.

## Woven (Fabric) Stitch

If you have odd yardages left over from sewing, they can be used with this stitch to create a knitted rug with a patchwork effect. Keep your knitted strips fairly narrow, (13 stitches works well). Knit 'blocks' of color into the rug by changing the color of the fabric strip often. For a large rug in a single color, use circular needles to knit the greatest width in a single row.

In planning your rug, allow 1¾ yards of 45-inch fabric cut 1½ inches wide and double folded for each square foot of the rug. Or,

## *The Woven (Fabric) Stitch*

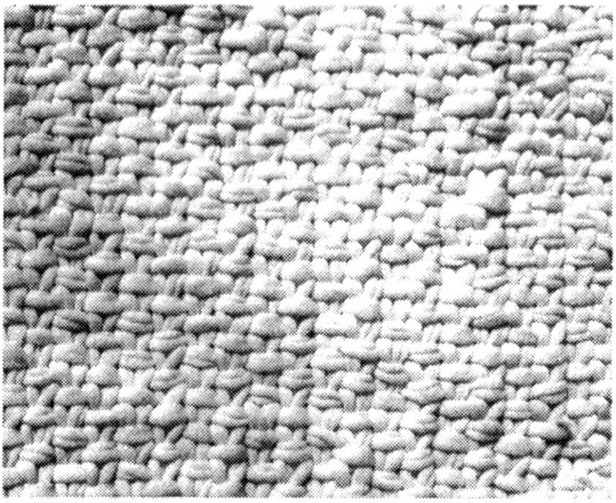

*Made with a single fabric strip, the woven or fabric stitch is the easiest way to achieve a woven look in a knitted rug.*

## *Cross-woven Knitted Rugs*

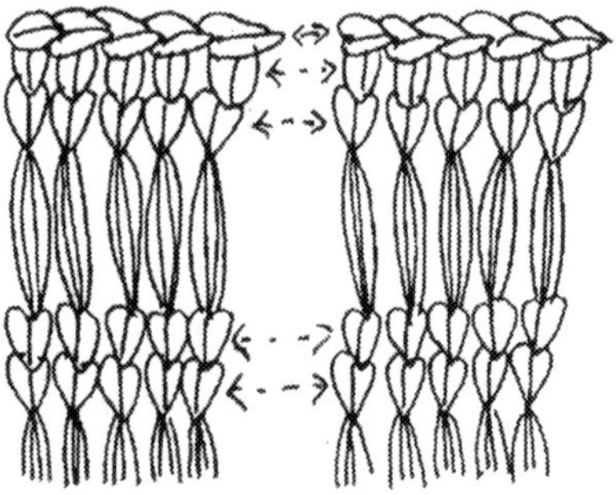

*Cross-woven knitted rugs are made in two steps. The knitting is first completed using the "drop" or "open stripe" stitch. Severals strips of knitting can be made and then joined togsether for the most intersting effects. Last, the unknitted portions are cross-woven also using fabric strip. Below is a detail of the completed knitting before cross-weaving.*

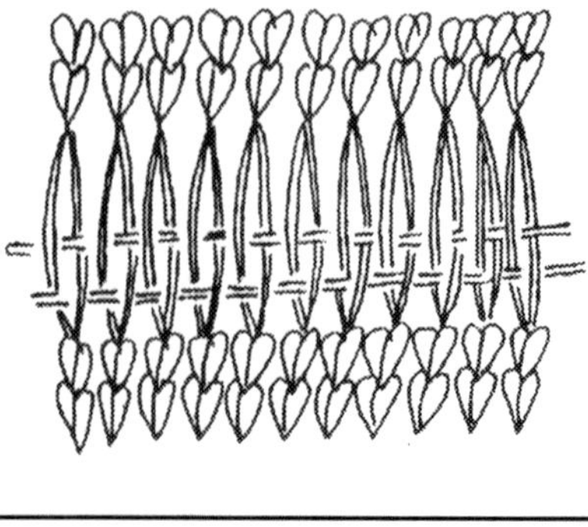

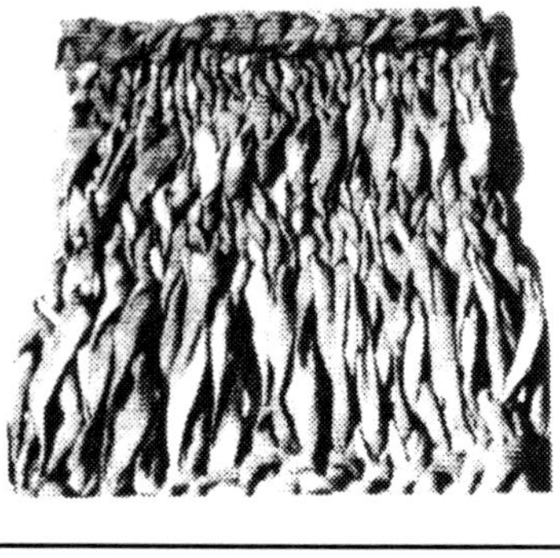

allow 1¼ yards of light woven cottons (45-inch) or 7/8 yards of single-knit cotton T-shirt fabric, cut 1 inch wide for each square foot. Single knit fabrics work well in this method as do the pre-folded strips since they both will accent the woven appearance.

Using size 15 needles (10 mm), the approximate gauge for this stitch is: 12 rows = 3 inches; and 6 stitches = 3 inches. Note that you really should do a small practice piece with this stitch before you begin your rug. It will take a little repetition before you have the rhythm, then your rug making will proceed more quickly.

**Directions:**

Cast on an odd number of stitches.

**Row 1:** Knit 1 *Bring strip to front of work, then Slip one stitch. Take strip to back of work, then Knit 1* Repeat the sequence between the * across row

**Row 2:** Knit 1, Purl 1, *Take strip to back of work, then slip one stitch. Bring strip to the front, then Purl 1* Repeat * across row until the last stitch. Knit 1 in last stitch.

**Repeat** Rows 1 and 2 until work reaches desired length.

To end the rug, casting off is done after a Row 2. Cast off knitwise and lace the sections together following the general directions for strip construction.

**Knitting with Weaving in the Rug**

This method is similar to the woven stitch above with the exception that the weaving is done with a second fabric instead of the knitting strip. This allows for some flexibility in material and color selection that isn't practical otherwise. The knitted base can be of an entirely different fabric—or even yarn. For weaving, heavy fabrics such as woolens can be used which are otherwise not easily incorporated into flat knitted rugs. Note that if you do choose a yarn for the knitting, it should be a fairly bulky weight. Thin yarns tend to sink into the weaving strip, making it hard to adjust the stitching to evenness in the early rows.

Plan to knit this rug in a single section if at all possible. Before you begin, you will also need to decide whether you want a finished edge all around the rug or fringes at the ends of the row. If you want a finished edge the fabric strip that is chosen for weaving should be joined to a continuous strip and rolled into a ball. For fringes, the weaving strips can be cut from yard goods allowing for the width of the knitting plus the length of the desired fringes (and some goof allowance—2 inches in the example). For example, if the width of the knitting is 30 inches, and the fringes will be 3 inches on each side, cut the fabric strip for weaving 30 + 3 + 3 + 2 = 38 inches. Knitting is done with plain stockinette stitch.

**Directions**

Use size 15 (10 mm) circular needles

Cast on the desired number of stitches. For a tabby weave, an odd number of stitches is best.

**Row 1**: Knit 1, lay the weaving strip between the needles with the longest end toward the back. Knit 1, bring the weaving strip to the front of the work. Knit 1, bring the weaving strip to the back of the work. Repeat across the row moving the weaving strip alternately to the front and back with each stitch.

**Row 2**: Purl 1, lay the weaving strip between the needles with the longest end toward the back. Purl 1, bring the weaving strip to the front of the work. Purl 1, bring the weaving strip to the back. Repeat across the row moving the weaving strip alternately to the front and back with each stitch.

Rows 1 and 2 are alternated to complete the rug. Note that for the first several rows you will need to adjust the stitches along the weaving strip to an even spacing. Once the knitting is about a foot long, the stitches will be more cooperative in their positions and you won't have to readjust as often.

When the rug reaches the desired length, cast off. Then lay the rug flat and readjust any more stitch positions so that it is even and square. Trim the fringes with a straight edge. If your weaving strip is fairly bulky you may need to hand sew along the fringes at the edge of the knitting to get them to lay flat. Steaming with an iron and pressing cloth will also settle most fringes.

For a finished edge, the weaving strip is brought around the last knitted stitch in the first row to begin the second row of knitting. With a finished edge you must adjust the knitted stitches for evenness on each row.

The directions above will produce a tabby weave, but other weaves are possible including simple twills. A striped effect is produced if the weaving strip is to the same side on subsequent rows. Experiment with sample pieces before beginning a rug since different fabrics will create different effects in the rug.

## Cross-woven Knitted Rugs

Another novel type of knitted rug is the cross-woven rug. They can be knit in a single piece or as a strip rug. The 'drop' or 'open-stripe' stitch is used to knit sections that alternately have stockinette and sections of strip that aren't knitted. After the rug strips are knitted and assembled, these open sections are cross-woven with other fabrics. This produces a rug with two distinct textures.

Use calico, broadcloth or any shirt-weight fabric for both the knitting and the weaving. Cut the strips 1½ inches wide and double-fold them. Torn strips will not handle well and single knit fabrics stretch too much and will tend to distort the finished rug. If you want a contemporary look in the rug, use only one fabric for both the knitting and the weaving. This accents the textures. For a county look, knit each strip in a different color, and weave with a mix of colors in a hit or miss selection.

The cross-woven knitted rug is created in three steps: 1) knitting the strips for the rug base; 2) assembling the strips; and 3) cross-weaving the entire rug. Optional fringes can be added to the end of the rug and the edges of the knitting.

### Step 1 Knitting the Strips for the Rug Base.

Rug sections can be knit in any desired width.
Cast on the desired number of stitches.
Row 1: Purl across.
Row 2: Wind strip around needle, then knit 1. Repeat this with each stitch across row.
Row 3: Purl across, letting the wrapped loops drop.
Row 4: Knit across
Repeat rows 1 though 4, until work reaches desired length. End with a purl row and cast off.

**For wider bands of knitting** in the finished rug, simply increase the rows of knitting before your wrap/drop sequences. The pattern as given creates 4 rows of stockinette between the open sections. You can increase the numbers of knitted rows as you wish—just make sure that each knitted section matches other rug sections you knit.

**For wider bands of weaving,** in Row 2, wrap the strip around the needle more than once. One wrap around the needle will yield a 1-inch weaving section; two wraps gives about a 2-inch weaving space; and three wraps gives about a 3-inch weaving space. Always use the same number of wraps in each stitch across the row, and in all corresponding rug sections.

**Step 2: Assemble the Rug Sections.**

When all rug sections have been knitted, they should be laid side by side, with the stitching oriented in the same direction. Lace the knitted rows of adjacent sections together, using the same fabric strip as was used for the knitting. Sew down the ends of the lacing. The lacing should be snug so that the sections are firmly joined, but not so tight as to buckle the knitting.

**Step 3: Cross-weaving the Knitted Rug.**

The fabric strips that you will weave with should be cut at least six inches longer than the width of the rug. The extra length will form the fringes at the sides of the rug. Work on a table and weave through the open areas of the rug. A large-eye lacing or weaving needle will make the work go more quickly. Weave strips through each section until the area is firm. The knitting should not be affected. If you have trouble weaving a final strip, it is likely that you already have sufficient strips woven in that section. Don't force the weaving.

After a section is completely cross-woven, adjust the strands, both horizontal and vertical, with your fingers so that the weaving is even and the section lays flat. Then proceed to weaving the next section.

After all sections are cross-woven, sew around the outside edge with needle and thread. Firmly stitch the fringe to the outside strand of the rug. Fringes can be added at the ends of the rug, and along the edges of the knitted portions, using the fabric strip as well. See the Handbook section for a discussion of fringes.

**Knitting a Soumak Weave**

This technique evolved while experimenting with various knitted structures to mimic a Berber carpet texture with knitting. Though the Berber texture didn't result, this method does create an interesting raised surface and narrow stripes if two different fabrics are used. The internal structure in profile is the same as the Japanese Soumak weave, replacing the warp threads on the loom with knitted stitches. It may seem a little confusing to the non-structuralist to call this a weave of any sort since the processes are all familiar knitting procedures done in an unusual order and using two fabrics simultaneously, but the internal structures are so closely related that this type of rug can almost qualify as off-loom weaving.

This method is most easily learned with two fabrics of different colors and a practice piece is a necessity before beginning a rug. Most likely you will be tempted to use bulky yarns for this method since it is a good medium for experimentation and you don't have to fuss with preparing the fabric. That is actually a good thing since this method produces a thicker and sturdier knitted rug than plain knitting with yarn, so it is actually very well suited to the use of bulky yarns.

As you plan this type of rug, keep in mind that it is the fabric which is used for the cast-on, cast-off series that will show most prominently in the surface. This fabric forms the "shoulders" of the ridges. The fabric used for the knitting shows only at the "peak" of the ridges.

**Practice:** Use size 15 (10 mm) knitting needles. Choose two fabrics of the same weight and texture. Cut and double-fold lightweight woven cottons (1½ inches wide) or cotton single knit fabrics one inch wide. Cast on the desired number of stitches using the light fabric on the left needle. Cast on one stitch of the dark fabric on the right needle. (See photo.) The knitting will be done with the fabric on the left needle. The dark fabric on the right needle is only cast on and cast off, never actually knitted.

For purposes of clarity, I'll refer to the two fabrics as the "light" fabric and the "dark" fabric corresponding to the illustration. Slip the first stitch of the light fabric onto the right needle. Then

## *Knitting a Soumak Weave*

*In profile, a soumak weave has the weft threads wound once around each warp thread. In this style of knitting the "cast on-cast off" fabric creates the same profile around the knitted stitches.*

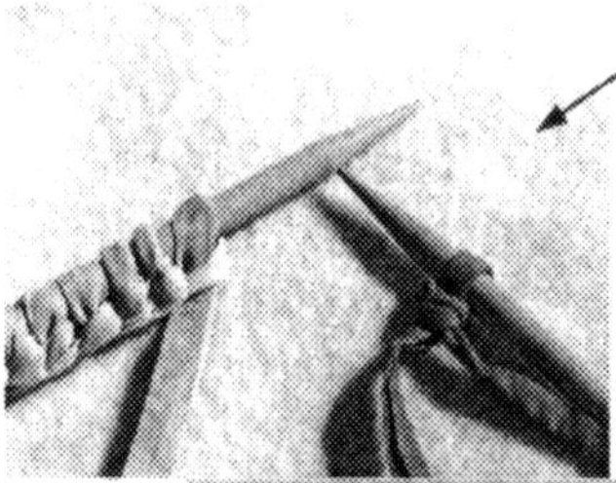

*Cast on the desired number of stitches on the left needle and only one stitch on the right needle.*

*Knit the first stitch as usual.*

*Then cast off from the right needle as shown with the dark fabric.*

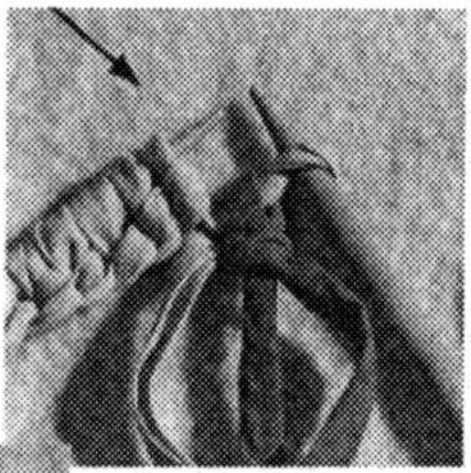

*Next complete sequence:*

*Cast on (dark fabric), Knit 1 (light fabric), Cast off (dark fabric). Below are several rows showing the striped effect created.*

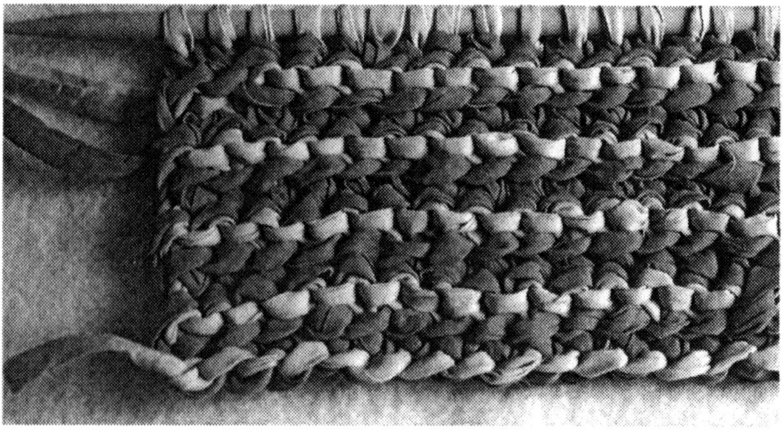

pull the dark fabric over and off (like casting off) so that only the light fabric remains on the needle. Then cast on one with the dark fabric onto the right needle. Knit one with the light fabric. You'll have one dark loop on the right needle. Pull it up and over the light stitch (cast off). There should be two light stitches remaining on the right needle.

Repeat:

Cast on—dark fabric

Knit one—light fabric

Cast off—dark fabric

That sequence completes one stitch. Work across the row in the same manner. (This is a great excuse to talk to yourself while you get the rhythm "Cast on, Knit, Cast off" and is really helpful too.)

When you reach the end of the first row, turn the work. To begin the second row, cast on one stitch with the dark fabric on the right needle. Knit the first light stitch, then cast off the dark fabric. Complete the row as you did the first.

After you've completed several rows of the practice piece, you should have the rhythm of the process and you can pull it apart and start a rug. You can accent the raised rows by using two different strips of the same fabric, but you really have to pay attention to keep the one that is knitted separate from the one that is just cast on and cast off.

If you're looking for a rug in which the ridges run along its length, use a long pair of circular needles to allow the rug to be knitted in one piece. Cast on enough stitches so that you are knitting along the length of the rug. That way the narrow stripes that appear in the knitting will run the length of the rug instead of across the width. (Also see the Chapter on knitting rugs in one piece for more information.)

## CHAPTER 14

# *Knitting Designs into a Rug*

In the very first edition of *Knitted Rag Rugs for the Craftsman*, I'd included a section on how to knit patterns into rugs. I'd made the unjustified assumption that people were familiar with the *intarsia* technique, which really hadn't come into general use at that time. In the second edition, I'd just dropped that section because people had so much trouble with the concept. Now, however, there are a number of good knitting references and even entire books that have been written about intarsia, so here we are again.

With intarsia, there is a separate source of yarn/strip for each color change in the knitted design. This is quite different than the Fair Isle type of knitting where strands of yarn are simply strung along the back of the work to their next use in the pattern. Intarsia is feasible with fabric strip with a few modifications from the yarn method. The stockinette and garter stitches are really the only practical stitches for intarsia with fabric, so don't worry about elaborations.

If once you get familiar with the basics of knitting with fabric strips, you want to try knitting in a pattern, the biggest challenge that you will have to make is having two, three, four or more balls of strip to keep straight. Fabric strip is so much more bulky than yarn that it can't be wound around a bobbin as can yarns. By itself, that is often enough of a problem to be discouraging. The best way to deal with tangling is to have a separate container for each ball. A small box or plastic bin will work fine. At the end of each row, you will have to realign the containers to the order in which the fabrics will be used in the row to be knitted. (Yes, every row. Don't skip it or the strip will tangle and create a much larger problem.)

Also, simply due to the bulk of fabric strip, it is impractical to develop the elaborate types of designs that are possible with yarns. Plan your designs so that you have at most four color changes (5 different fabric strips), and for your first piece you should have at most two color changes (3 different colored fabric strips).

Another difference in working with fabric strip is that at the point of color changes, the pattern should not be shifted more than two stitches at a time and one is better. Shifting by more stitches than that will create a loose spot on the surface of the rug. That limitation also narrows the options for designs that can be knitted with fabric strip. Designs based on diagonal lines work best (diagonal stripes, chevrons, diamonds, etc.).

As you begin or end a color, leave a tail of fabric strip hanging about six inches from the rug. These are worked back into the rug after the knitting is completed.

Small details are not feasible in intarsia with fabric strip, but within reason, they can be added using the "duplicate stitch" type of embroidery. These need to be small areas since the duplicate stitch will create a thicker spot on the rug and will be subject to wear. (If you're making a wall hanging the duplicate stitch can be used freely since surface wear isn't a factor.)

To begin a section of intarsia knitting, cast on stitches using only a single fabric. The most solid rug will result if you knit at least an inch or two of stockinette (or garter) stitch with just the first color. When you are ready to knit the first row in which a color change occurs, knit across to the point of the new color. Then simply knit with the new strip leaving about six inches loose at the beginning. Work that color in accordance with your design, then begin with the next in the same way, just leaving a section of fabric strip hanging loose. Note that with each color change a new ball of strip is begun. Never drag one strip across the back of the rug—begin with a new ball instead.

## CHAPTER 15

# *Knitting Rugs in One Piece*

There is an obvious advantage in being able to knit a rug in a single piece. There are no sections to join and, with most stitch patterns, no finishing to worry about. As soon as the rug comes off the needles, it is ready to use. Of course the disadvantage is that the knitting can become heavy with a very large rug. Therefore a compromise should be kept in mind for extremely large rugs; knit a largish center section and add knitted borders for a room-size rug.

From a design standpoint, knitting in one piece allows for several options in shaping the rug and also opens the possibility of having stripes running the length of the rug instead of across the width. Fairly large rugs can be knitted in one piece using circular needles or needle extenders. Most commercially made circular needles have about a 3-foot length, so for a larger dimension you may need to manufacture your own long needles (see the Handbook section for how).

### Knitting Rectangular Rugs as a Single Piece

Knitting rectangular rugs in a single section is just a matter of casting on the number of stitches needed and knitting away. You can knit across the width of the rug, or along the length. This is a good procedure for some of the shaggy rugs or those with textural stitches (shingle, corn-on-the-cob). With a lot of stitches on the needle, the standard method of casting on can lead to a loose edge, however, so it is recommended that you cast on using one of the alternate methods in the Handbook section. The alternate casting-on methods also will minimize the curl that sometimes occurs with the stockinette and related stitches.

This will seem obvious to experienced knitters, but for a large rug, check your gauge before you begin. Using the same fabric and needles that you intend to use for your rug, knit a sample piece at least 10 stitches wide and 10 rows long. Then measure how many stitches are equivalent to an inch so that you know how many will have to be cast on. Also, measure the knitted rows so that you will have an approximate idea of how many rows will be knitted.

Rectangular rugs just three feet across will get heavy after awhile and since you will be handling the weight a lot, don't make your knitting a marathon event. Take breaks frequently and stretch your neck and shoulders. If you find yourself sitting with your head bent over the work, put a pillow in your lap to raise the rug to a more livable height. If you already have problems with your wrists from repetitive motion sorts of injuries, approach a large rug with extra caution. Don't even try to work on it more often than every other day. Actually, if you have this sort of injury it is a much better choice to work on a strip or block rug that can be done in sections that weigh a whole lot less.

Beginners often make the mistake of starting right off on a large rug, then they get discouraged and leave the project half-finished. Start small—for instance with a bathmat project that will work along fast enough to keep your interest. If you decide later to make it a bigger rug, the small project can be used as the center of a block or strip rug. With a rectangular rug, knitted strips can be added on all four sides.

I haven't given any fabric requirements in this chapter since there are so many possibilities. Instead consult the handbook section for the type of fabric that you'll want to use to calculate how much your particular rug will need. Then add 10% to that amount. There is nothing more maddening than coming up just a little, tiny bit short. If you've got fabric left over, you can always make a small coordinating project (like a basket).

## Knitting an Oval Rug in a Single Section

Particularly in high traffic areas, oval rugs are a more practical shape than rectangular ones. Ovals don't have corners, which seem to be prone to curling up when folks drag their feet just a little. (In fact it was to overcome that particular problem in rectangular rugs that I developed the shingle pattern stitch several years back.)

Oval rugs are knitted by gradually increasing the width of the knitting at the beginning forming a gentle curve, and then decreasing in the same fashion at the other end. In between the curved sections are rows of straight knitting, and of course, the longer straight section is, the longer the oval will be.

I'm going to give two sets of directions for making an oval. The first set is for beginners and is much easier to follow, although the oval shape isn't perfectly rounded. Instead it is squared off so that the rug looks like a hexagonal-oval. These are the types of ovals to begin with and the angular sections will become less pronounced if another round of knitting is added to the outside. Some people actually prefer this hexagonal-oval because it does have an old fashioned look. The hexagonal-oval is also an ideal shape for a long hall runner.

With both of the oval patterns you'll need to know how many stitches to cast on for the width of the rug you want. With most light cottons on size 15 needles, you'll have 2.3 to 2.5 stitches per inch. So for example, if you want to knit a rug 24 inches wide, figure on a total of 55 to 60 stitches. A third of that number will be cast on to begin a hexagonal-oval and a fourth of that number will be needed to cast on for the regular oval.

## General Directions for Knitting a Hexagonal-Oval Rug in One Piece

The directions below are written for the garter stitch. I'm assuming here that if you've decided to take on a large rug in a different stitch that you will modify the directions as needed. For example, for a stockinette rug, alternate rows will need to have purled stitches instead of the knit ones. Use size 15 (10 mm) circular knitting needles.

*Knitting the first end*: Cast on the number of stitches that would be needed to knit one third (1/3) of the width of the rug.

Row 1: Slip 1, Knit 1, cast on 1 on the working needle, then knit to the end of the row.

## *Knitting Rugs in a Single Piece*

*The easiest shape of rug to knit in a single section is a rectangular rug, and the hardest is a true oval. In between there are two more unusual shapes: the hexagonal-end oval and the ovoid shapes. Both require circular needles or needle extensions to knit.*

*The hexagonal-end oval, shown above in progress, is begun by casting on stitches to knit 1/3 of the width of the finished rug. Increases are made in each row to reach the final rug width. The process is reversed at the other end.*

*An ovaid rug has rounded, pointy ends and can be made short to approximate a rounded diamond shape or into a longer runner. With both the hexagonal oval and the ovoid shapes, rounds of knitting can be added to the outside which will soften the angles of the shape, and of course, make a larger rug.*

Repeat this row, casting on one stitch each time until the knitting reaches the desired width of the rug.

*Knitting the body of the rug:* This is completed in plain knitting with no increases or decreases. (Slip 1, Knit across.) When the rug reaches the desired length, you are ready to knit the other end. Remember in figuring the length that just as much length will be taken up by the final end as the first end.

*Knitting the final end:* In each row there will be one less stitch than in the previous row. This is done by knitting two stitches together. This is done for each row: Slip 1, Knit 1, Knit 2 together, then knit across to the end of the row. When the number of stitches is reduced to the same number that you had originally cast on, it is time to cast off to end the rug.

**General Directions for Knitting an Oval Shape in One Piece**

Keep a pencil and paper handy because you're going to have to count rows and keep track of which row you are on.

Use size 15 (10 mm) circular knitting needles.

*First curved end*: Cast on sufficient stitches to knit one-fourth of the width of the rug.

Rows 1 through 6: Slip 1, Knit 1, Cast on one stitch onto right needle, Knit 1, Cast on one stitch onto the right needle. Then knit to the end of the row. (There are two increases in each row.)

Rows 7 through 10: Slip 1, Knit 1, Cast on 1. Then knit to the end of the row. (There is one increase in each row.)

Rows 11 and 12: Slip 1, Knit 1, Cast on 1. Then knit to the end of the row.

Rows 13 and 14: Slip 1, Knit across.

Rows 15 and 16: Slip 1, Knit 1, Cast on 1. Then knit to the end of the row.

Row 17 on: You'll be inserting an increase only in row numbers that are divisible by 3, from this point until the rug reaches its final width.

So for rows not divisible by 3: Slip 1, Knit across.

For rows which are divisible by 3: Slip 1, Knit 1, Cast on 1, then knit to the end of the row. It is helpful to mark the row with the cast on stitch so that you don't have to recount all of the rows each time. Also, make a note of the row number of the last row in which you added a stitch. You'll need to know that number to work the other end of the rug.

*Straight knitted section.* Once your knitting reaches the desired width of the rug, measure the length of the knitting that you have done so far and write it down. The final end will take just as much length to form the curve so you will need to allow for it. Continue the rug by adding as many rows of plain knitting (Slip 1, Knit Across) as it takes to get your rug to the length that you want. The length of the first curved end plus the *total length* that you have knitted should equal the final length that you want the rug to be.

*Final curved section.* When your straight knitting is as long as you want, the ending curve is formed by knitting two stitches together in the appropriate rows. To save your sanity, make a checklist with the row numbers listed in reverse order. The first number should be the same as the last row that had a stitch cast on. For example if the last row with a cast on was row 39, begin your numbering with that and number in descending order (39, 38, 37, 36, etc.). Highlight the rows that will have a decrease (two stitches knitted together). These are:

Rows 31 and higher, decrease one in row numbers divisible by 3; : Slip 1, Knit 2 together, knit across

Rows 11 through 16, decrease one in alternate pairs of rows; : Slip 1, Knit 2 together, knit across

Rows 7 through 10, decrease one in every row; and : Slip 1, Knit 2 together, knit across

Rows 1 through 6, two decreases in every row. Slip 1, Knit 2 together, Knit 1, Knit 2 together, knit across.

In each of the highlighted rows on your list, you will decrease one stitch by knitting two stitches together. After you complete Row 1, there should be the same number of stitches remaining on the needle as were originally cast on. To finish up the rug cast off these last stitches. Then lace the end of the strip into the rug (at both ends) and secure it with hand sewing so it doesn't work loose in laundering. Clip off any excess.

## Knitting an Ovoid Rug

An ovoid rug is made on the same principle as the oval but is a narrower shape. Since the ovoid pattern doesn't require that you keep track of row numbers, so it is a good choice to begin knitting rugs in one piece with rounded ends. If you add bordering rows of knitting to the ovoid shape, it will begin to be more oval with each row added. So, if you are using the ovoid as a beginning project, plan to make it fairly small so that you get the feel of the technique. Then if you want a larger rug, additional rounds of knitting can be added to it.

.

**Basic Directions for an Ovoid Rug:**

Use size 15 (10 mm) circular knitting needles.
Cast on 8 stitches
Slip 1, Knit 7, Cast on 1, turn work
Slip 1, Knit 8, Cast on 1, turn work
Slip 1, Knit 9, Cast on 1, turn work

This pattern is continued with each subsequent row beginning with Slip 1, then Knit across to the end, and cast on 1 stitch at the beginning of each row. Just keep casting on one stitch in each row until your rug reaches the width that you want. Then make the center section of the rug with straight knitting (Slip 1, Knit across each row) until you have the length that you want. Remember that the decreasing at the other end will take as many rows as the increasing did and that length should be taken into account in deciding when to begin decreasing.

When your straight knitting is as long as you want, the ending curve is formed by knitting two stitches together (decrease 1) in each row until only 8 stitches are left. These rows are knitted: Slip 1, Knit 2 together, knit across. When there are only 8 stitches remaining, cast off. Lace the end of the strip into the rug (at both ends) and secure it with hand sewing so it doesn't work loose in laundering. Clip off any excess.

# CHAPTER 16

# *Knitted Rag Baskets and Other Small Projects*

The following projects are recommended for beginners. They are small and quickly made. If you want to make a matching set, be sure to purchase enough fabric of the same color to complete all of the pieces. (Fabric requirements shown for one item.) Since kitchen items will need regular washing, be sure to select washable fabrics. For items which will be exposed to high heat be sure that cotton makes up at least 75% of the fiber content.

## Knitted Hotpads

Hotpads are thick (like a mini-rug) and are used to set hot pans and dishes on the table. (Potholders are thinner and more flexible. They are used to protect your hands when grasping hot dishes.)

These hotpads will provide a little practice with knitting with fabric so that you can approach rug making with confidence. Hotpads are the same weight as knitted rugs, and you'll be able to see and feel the texture of knitted rugs in the finished project. Since kitchen items will need regular washing, be sure to select washable fabrics. Hotpads will be exposed to high temperatures which can melt synthetics, so make sure that the fabric you choose has cotton for at least 75% of the fiber content.

## *Knitting Small Items and Rag Baskets*

*Small knitted projects are ideal for beginning knitters and those learning to knit with fabric strip. The hotpads shown at left are a sampling of simple projects that make wonderful gifts or items for sale. Shown are the heart shaped and round hot pads and the square hotpad done both with the garter stitch (left) and the shingle pattern (right).*

*Knitted baskets are made in two pieces. First the base of the basket is knitted in the desired shape. A round base is shown.*

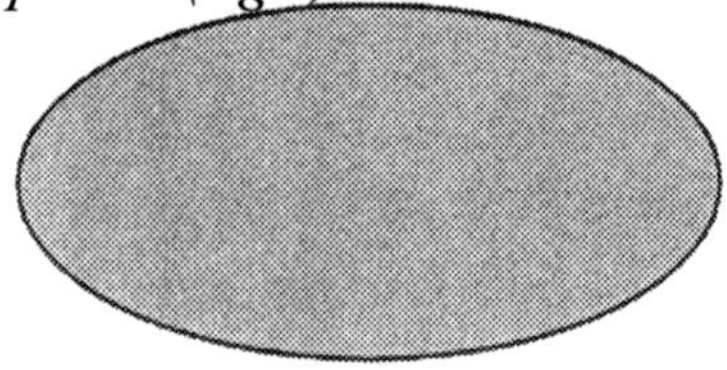

*Then the side piece is knitted as a single section to fit around the outside of the base.*

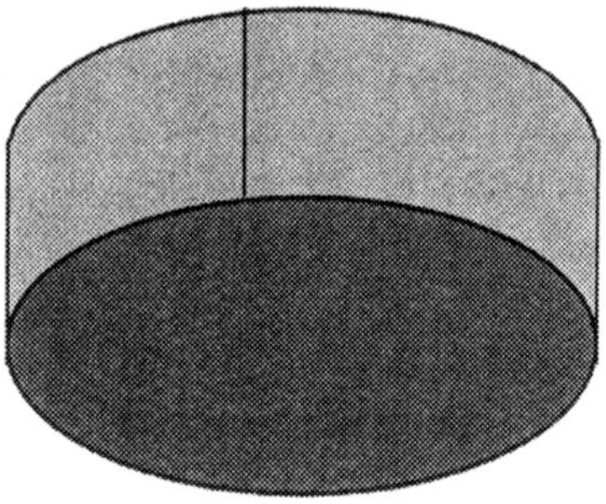

*The two pieces are then laced together to form the basket itself. Below are the top and bottom views of a round knitted basket (made from a T-shirt knit fabric) using this two-part construction.*

**Basic Square (8" x 8") Hotpad**

You will find that this project makes up quickly and that the hotpad is very useful by itself. Don't be surprised if you find yourself making several of these for friends. For gifts, the shingle pattern stitch has a much fancier look so give it a try with these square hotpads also.

For each hotpad allow ½ yard of 60-inch wide single-knit T-shirt fabric. Cut strips one inch wide. For woven cottons, allow ¾ yard of 45-inch wide fabric cut into strips 1½ inches wide and double-fold to hide the raw edges.

**Directions**

Cast on 18 stitches.
*Slip 1, Knit 17*
Repeat until 32 rows are complete.
Cast off.

**Finishing.** Use a large-eye lacing needle to lace the ends of the fabric strip back into the work. Sew the ends in place and clip off any excess. Size of the finished hotpad will vary slightly depending on the fabric used. If you want to be able to hang the hotpad on the wall when not in use, simply sew a loop of the extra fabric strip to one corner.

**8" Round Hotpad**

The circle is formed by knitting repeated series of partial rows which form 'wedges'. (This is the same pattern used for the center of the 'bullseye' and wedge knitted rugs.) For a plain hotpad use a single fabric for the entire project. For a fancy hotpad, knit each wedge with a different color of fabric (or alternate two fabrics for the wedges).

For each hotpad allow ½ yard of 60-inch wide single-knit T-shirt fabric. Cut strips one inch wide. For woven cottons, allow ¾ yard of 45-inch wide fabric cut into strips 1½ inches wide and double-folded to hide the raw edges.

**Directions**

Cast on 8 stitches
Row 1: Knit 2, turn work
Row 2: Slip 1, Knit 1, turn work
Row 3: Knit 4, turn work
Row 4: Slip 1, Knit 3, turn work

Row 5: Knit 6, turn work
Row 6: Slip 1, Knit 5, turn work
Row 7: Knit 8, turn work
Row 8: Slip 1, Knit 7, turn work

Rows 1 through 8 make one 'wedge.' Repeat these rows in sequence twelve times to make a full circle.

On the 12th repetition, don't knit row 8—cast off as you knit row 7. This will leave the last stitch at the center of the circle. Pull the fabric strip up through the last stitch and cut off the rug strip about 18 inches from the work. You will use this strip to lace the edges of the circle together.

**Finishing.** Thread the end of the strip into a large-eye lacing needle. Begin lacing the circle by passing the needle through the center stitches and pull up snugly so the center of the circle is closed. Then whip-stitch the edges of the circle together. The lacing should be done snugly, but not so tightly that the shape of the circle is distorted. When lacing is complete, work the end of the fabric strip back into the knitting, sew in place and clip off any excess.

**Heart Hotpad (9¼ " x 8")**

This hotpad has a true heart shape and makes a very popular gift. Because of the shaping, this pattern is suitable for knitters familiar with increasing and decreasing.

**Directions**

Abbreviations: 'Inc' = Increase (for you beginners, increasing is done by casting on a stitch on the working needle. For right handed knitters, that is the right needle. For left handers, the working needle will be the left needle.)
'Knit 2 Tog' = Knit 2 Together (two stitches are knitted at the same time.)
Knitting is begun at the point of the heart.
Cast on 2
Row 1: Slip 1, Knit 1
Row 2: Slip 1, Inc 1, Knit1
Row 3: Slip 1, Knit 1, Inc 1, Knit 1
Row 4: Slip1, Knit 1, Inc 1, Knit 2
Row 5: Slip 1, Knit 2, Inc 1, Knit 2

Row 6: Slip1, Knit 2, Inc 1, Knit 3
Row 7: Slip 1, Knit 3, Inc 1, Knit 3
Row 8: Slip 1, Knit 3, Inc 1, Knit 4
Row 9: Slip 1, Knit 4, Inc 1, Knit 4
Row 10: Slip 1, Knit 4, Inc 1, Knit 5
Row 11: Slip 1, Knit 5, Inc 1, Knit 5
Row 12: Slip 1, Knit 5, Inc 1, Knit 6
Row 13: Slip 1, Knit 6, Inc 1, Knit 6
Row 14: Slip1, Knit 6, Inc 1, Knit 7
Row 15: Slip 1, Knit 7, Inc 1, Knit 7
Row 16: Slip 1, Knit 7, Inc 1, Knit 8
Row 17: Slip 1, Knit 8, Inc 1, Knit 8
Row 18: Slip 1, Knit 8, Inc 1, Knit 9
Row 19: Slip 1, Knit 9, Inc 1, Knit 9
Row 20: Slip 1, Knit 9, Inc 1, Knit 10
Row 21: Slip 1, Knit 10, Inc 1, Knit 10
Row 22: Slip 1, Knit 10, Inc 1, Knit 11
Row 23: Slip 1, Knit 11, Inc 1, Knit 11
Row 24: Slip 1, Knit 11, Inc 1, Knit 12
Row 25: Slip 1, Knit 12, Inc 1, Knit 12
Row 26: Slip 1, Knit 25

The 'body' of the heart is now complete and knitting proceeds individually on the lobes. While knitting the first lobe of the heart, thirteen stitches will remain unworked on one needle.
Row 27: Slip 1, Knit 12, turn work
Row 28: Slip 1, Knit 12, turn work
Row 29: Slip 1, Knit 12, turn work
Row 30: Slip 1, Knit 5, Knit 2 tog, Knit 5
Row 31: Slip 1, Knit 4, Knit 2 tog, Knit 5
Row 32: Slip 1, Knit 4, Knit 2 tog, Knit 4
Row 33: Slip 1, Knit 3, Knit 2 tog, Knit 4
Row 34: Slip 1, Knit 1, Knit 2 tog, Knit 1, Knit 2 tog, Knit 2
Row 35: Slip 1, Knit 2 tog, Knit 1, Knit 2 tog, Knit 1
Row 36: Knit 2 tog, Knit 2 tog, Knit 1
Row 37: Knit 2 tog, Knit 1
Cast off

Cut fabric strip about six inches from work. Lace the strip end back into knitting.

Using the fabric strip on the ball: pin the strip at the end of the thirteen unworked stitches, leaving about 6 inches for lacing back into the work.

Repeat Rows 27 through 37 with the stitches remaining on the needles to complete the second lobe of the heart. Lace strip ends into work, and hand sew in place. Clip off any excess.

**Potholders**

Unlike hotpads, potholders are flexible enough to pick up hot dishes or pans from the oven. Potholders should only be made of fabrics that contain at least 75% cotton fiber—synthetics can melt. For each potholder allow ¾ yard of 45-inch wide fabric. Cut or tear strips one inch wide and do not fold the raw edges over. Note that all of the potholder patterns use Size 10 (6 mm) knitting needles in order to create a tight surface.

**Basic Square Stockinette Potholder**

This potholder is the thinnest and most flexible of the knitted potholders. It can be made with a crocheted edge or with a bound edge. One-hundred percent cotton fabric is best.

**Directions:**

Cast on 23 stitches

Row 1: Slip 1, Knit 22

Row 2: Slip 1, Purl 22

Repeat rows 1 and 2 until a total of 25 rows are completed (ending with a knitted row).

Cast off

If you want a bound edge on your potholder, pull the end of the fabric strip up through last stitch to secure it. Make sure you have sufficient fabric strip left for whichever edging you choose: for a bound edge allow 1½ yards of strip; for a single crochet edge allow 4 yards of strip; for a double crochet edge allow 8 yards of strip.

**Directions for bound edge.** Thread the end of the fabric strip into a large-eye lacing needle or weaving needle. Hold the hotpad so that the knitted side faces you. Insert one whip stitch or blanket stitch into each knitted stitch along the ends, and into each row on both sides of the potholder. When stitching is completed around the potholder, lace the end of the fabric strip into the knitting, secure the end with needle and thread, then clip off any excess. (See the Handbook section on Edging for more information.)

**Directions for single-crochet edge**. Use a size 'J' standard crochet hook. Insert the crochet hook into the final loop remaining after you have cast off the last row of purling. Chain 7 (for hanging loop). Insert the hook into first chain, chain 1. Single-crochet around the outside of the knitting, inserting one SC into each knitted stitch or row, and 3 SC into corner spaces. Slip stitch the strip to the hanging loop, and pull the end of the strip through the last stitch. Use a large-eye lacing needle to work the strip end into the knitting, secure the end with needle and thread, then clip off any excess.

**Basic Garter Stitch or Shingle Pattern Potholder**

The garter stitch and shingle pattern potholders are made with the same number of stitches and rows as stockinette potholder. They are slightly stiffer than the stockinette potholder, but work fine. (See the Handbook section for these stitch directions.)

**Knitted Placemats**

Knitted rag placemats are right at home on the table for a 'county' look. They are practical, and washable (just use washable fabrics for your strip). It is not recommended that you make placemats of 1½ inch double-folded strip, since they tend to be too thick to be practical. Instead use cotton fabrics cut or torn into ¾ inch strip, or one inch strip for very light fabrics. The basic placemat directions are for a rectangular shape, but you can use almost any of the basic rug patterns to make mini-rugs to use as placemats.

**Basic Placemat 12" x 18"**

Each placemat requires about 1¾ yards of 45" fabric. Cotton and cotton-blend woven fabrics (calico, muslin, broadcloth, etc.) are recommended. Use Size 10/ 6 mm knitting needles.

Cast on 34 stitches

Row 1: Slip 1, Knit 33

Row 2: Slip 1, Purl 33

Repeat rows 1 and 2 until 57 rows are complete, or until placemat measures 17 ¾ inches.
Cast off.
Edging is recommended for placemats to minimize any curl at the ends. Crocheted edges will lay flatter than bound edges. Follow the directions for edging for potholders.

**Serving Mat 12" x 18" Using T-shirt fabric**

This placemat/serving mat is thicker than the basic placemat pattern. It uses T-shirt single-knit fabric cut into one-inch strips. With the knitted border pattern the mat lays flat without edging. This mat is ideal for serving from large flat pans, such as lasagna dishes or large casseroles. Because of the border thickness, this mat is not recommended for placemats. Use cotton, single-knit (T-shirt) fabric. For each mat allow 1½ yards of 60-inch wide fabric. Cut strips 1 inch wide in the direction of the curl. Use size 15/ 10 mm knitting needles.

**Directions**

Cast on 30 stitches
Row 1: Slip 1, Knit 29
Row 2: Slip 1, Knit 29
Row 3: Slip 1, Knit 29
Row 4: Slip 1, Knit 29
Row 5: Slip 1, Knit 3, Purl 22, Knit 4
Row 6: Slip 1, Knit 29
Repeat Rows 5 and six until 46 rows are knitted, or until knitting measures 17 inches.
Last four rows: Repeat first four rows.
Cast off.
Lace ends of strip into the work, secure with hand sewing, clip off any excess.

**Making a Table-Runner**

Knitted table runners are both decorative and practical. They can serve as a table accent, and as a central 'hotpad' for serving from many hot dishes without damaging the tabletop. You can make a table runner by simply following the directions for either of the placemat patterns, and adjusting the length to suit your own desires.

Use the yardages for the placemats as a guide. For example, the placemats are 18" long. If you want a 36" table runner, double the yardage for the placemat. (If you make a table runner, buy extra matching fabric. From it cut 18-inch squares for napkins, and hem them on all four sides. This makes a very festive table setting.)

**Knitted Baskets**

'Rag' baskets are quite popular just now, and they can be knitted with fabric strip very simply. There are three basic construction methods. With the first, the base of the basket is knitted as a single unit—round, square, oval, rectangular, etc. Then a straight strip is knitted to fit around the base. The two sections are laced together to form the basket.

For a **round basket**, knit any round center (See wedge rug chapter). The side is made by knitting a straight strip, usually 12 stitches or wider in the garter stitch or shingle pattern. The strip is knit to fit, exactly around the center, and is simply laced to the round base. It is difficult to give a yardage figure for all baskets but for a typical 8 inch round basket, allow 2 yards of light cotton fabric cut into 1½ inch strip and double folded or 1½ yards of 60 inch wide T-shirt knit.

The same procedure is used for **other shapes**. For an oval basket, knit an oval base. For square or rectangular baskets, knit a square or rectangular base and then knit the side piece. The knitted section that forms the sides of the basket can be of any structural stitch (basically all of the stitches except stockinette and high-density stockinette).

The alternative methods are used only for square or rectangular baskets. To knit baskets in a single piece, a cross-shape is knitted and the corners laced to form the basket. You can extend the single piece of knitting to also include a handle.

You can also form a square or rectangular basket by knitting it in three sections. A straight section is knitted which will form the ends and the bottom of the basket. Then two pieces are knitted to form the sides of the basket and all three pieces are laced together. Use any of the structural knitting stitches in the Handbook sections for these baskets.

## *Knitting Square and Rectangular Baskets*

*The simplest way to knit a square or rectangular basket is to make it all in one piece.*

*1. Cast on stitches equal to the width of the basket.*
*2. Knit rows until the height of the basket is reached.*
*3. Cast on stitches equal to the height of the basket on both sides.*
*4. Knit rows until the length of the basket is reached.*
*5. Cast off stitches equal to the height of the basket on both sides.*
*6. Knit rows equal to the height of the basket (same as in #2).*
*7. Cast off stitches.*
*8. Lace the corners together.*

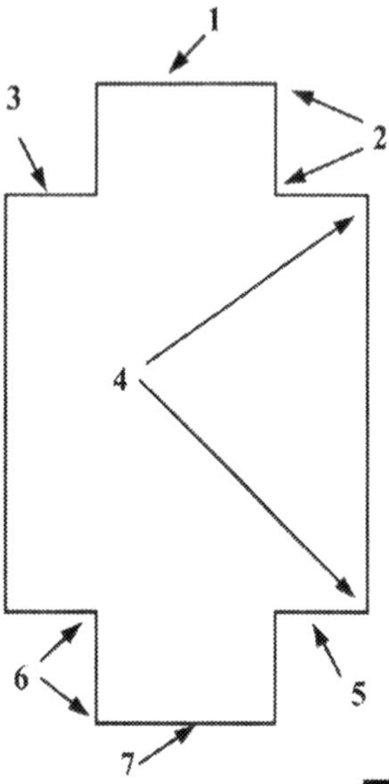

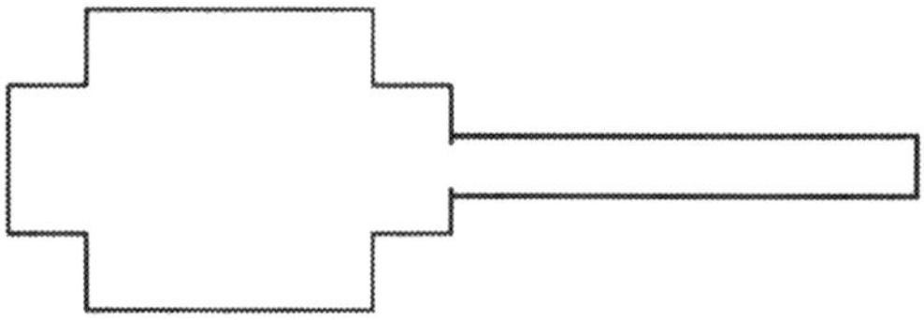

*You can knit a centered piece off the end to create a handle at the same time.*

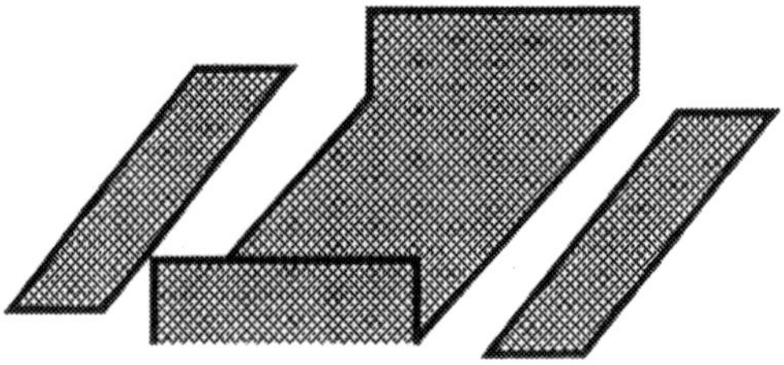

*A more complex basket assembly is done in three parts for baskets with squared corners. A central section is knitted which forms the base and both ends of the basket, and then the two sides of the basket are knit to fit the base. All three pieces are then laced together to form the basket. This assembly is more time consuming, but allows you to make the sides with different colors.*

**Basket handles** are optional, but can be made using the garter stitch. Simply knit a straight strip about 6 stitches wide and lace the ends to the sides of the basket. Handles that won't keep their shape can be reinforced by running a line of crochet slip stitches on the underside along both edges. Crochet slip stitches can be used also to stiffen the top edge of a basket.

**Basic Chairpad 16" x 16"**

This basic square chairpad will fit most types of kitchen chairs. If you have larger or smaller seats or a seat that is tapered, read over the directions then read the section on creating a custom chairpad. If you have several chairs that you want to make matching chair pads for, be sure to purchase sufficient fabric for all of them at the same time. If you have a chair in a bedroom, you might consider using sheets that match your linens.

**Fabric required.** Chairpads can be made of many different types of fabric. The yardages for the three most popular are: 3 yards of 60-inch wide T-shirt fabric (cut strips one inch wide so that edges curl under); 4½ yards of 45-inch wide cotton or cotton blend fabric (cut strips 1½ inches wide, and double-fold to hide raw edges); or 2¼ yards of 45-inch wide corduroy or denim (cut strips ¾ inch wide, and do not fold edges under). Use Size 15/ 10 mm knitting needles, 14 inches long for all fabrics.

**Directions for basic chairpad:**

Cast on 45 stitches

Row 1: Slip 1, Knit 44

Repeat Row 1 until 48 rows are completed, or until knitting measures 16 inches.

Cast off.

Lace ends of strip back into the work, and sew in place. Clip off any excess.

To make ties for chairpad. Cut two lengths of fabric strip, each 18 inches long. Lace the strip into the two back corners of the chairpad, so that they can be tied to the chair back. Edging a chairpad is optional, but a contrasting border will frame the knitting to show off your work. See the Handbook section for edgings.

## Making a Custom Size/Shape Chairpad

It is not often in knitting fabric projects that gauge is critical, but if you have an odd shaped chair, you'll want to check your gauge. The following directions are based on the gauge: 10 stitches = 4 inches; 12 rows = 4 inches. Because various fabrics will knit up slightly differently, you should check the gauge of the fabric strip you will be using, and alter the directions below as needed. If you are making a chairpad in excess of 18 inches in width, use circular knitting needles, since straight needles will overfill and be very difficult to handle.

### For a square or rectangular chairpad or benchpad

**Step 1:** Measure the chair you want to fit.
**Step 2:** Use the following formula to determine your knitting pattern:
Chair width (in inches) multiplied by 2.5 = Number of stitches to cast on
Desired pad length (in inches) multiplied by 3 = Number of Rows to knit.
**Step 3:** To determine how much fabric you will need:
Multiply the pad length times the width.
Divide this number by 224
Look up the yardage required for a standard 16" chairpad in your desired fabric and multiply it by the number above.

### For a tapering chairpad (for 'captains' style chairs):

**Step 1:** Measure the chair you want to fit.
**Step 2:** Use the following formula to determine your knitting pattern
Back chair width (in inches) multiplied by 2.5 = Number of stitches to cast on
Front chair width (in inches) multiplied by 2.5 = Number of stitches in final rows of knitting.
Desired pad length (in inches) multiplied by 3 = Number of rows of knitting.
**Step 3:** You now know that you will need to add stitches as you knit, to make the front edge wider than the back edge. Divide the total number of rows of knitting by the number of stitches you have to add. This number will tell you the number of rows between added stitches.

For example: A chair pad that measures 16 inches at the back edge and 20 inches at the front edge, and is 18 inches deep.

16 x 2.5 = 40 (Cast on 40 stitches)
20 x 2.5 = 50 (Last rows of knitting will have 50 stitches
50 - 40 = 10 (In the process of knitting, you will need to cast on 10 stitches)
18 x 3 = 54 (There will be 54 rows of knitting)
54 divided by 10 = 5.4 (You will want to add a stitch about every 5th row)
Note: Stitches are added at the center of the pad, not at the edges. This keeps the edges straight.

To calculate the yardage for a tapering chairpad, follow the same procedure as for square or rectangular pads. Use the average width of the pad for multiplying.

**Chairpads with Other Stitches**

Chairpads can be made with any of the alternate stitch patterns, but if you want to really pad the seat, select the raised types of stitches. The double-sided garter stitch will make the softest chairpad since foam can be inserted into the chairpad to provide extra cushioning. (See the Handbook section for the stitch directions.)

## CHAPTER 17

# *A Word About Using Yarns Instead of Fabric Strip*

(From the Second Edition of *Knitted Rag Rugs for the Craftsman*)

*Anyone familiar with my previous books on traditional American rugs knows my prejudice against modifying these techniques to accommodate modern yarns. Well, OK, I've mellowed some over the years and particularly with knitted rugs. All of the patterns in this book can be made with yarns, and they do make stunning rugs or afghans.*

*If you don't have the time to prepare your own fabric strip, yarns make a good starting place into the world of knitted rugs. To make rugs in the same sizes as the patterns used in this book, use size 15 (10 mm) needles, and knit with a very bulky wool yarn or four strands of worsted weight yarns at the same time.*

*To modify the patterns to make afghans, use Size 8 or Size 10 needles with a single strand of worsted weight yarn. For really stunning effects, the best patterns to use for afghans are the hexagon (pieced like a "Grandmother's Flower Garden" quilt) or the winding path. Block patterns can be made to resemble the "Log Cabin" type quilt. If you use long circular needles, you can use the wedge pattern (and a number of stitches divisible by 4) to make a six foot round afghan, with 24 'fans'.*

Well, that's what I'd written in the 1996 edition. The interest in using yarns and roving in knitted rugs hasn't gone away, so I thought I'd add a few more considerations for those who are interested in those materials.

First of all, part of my prejudices with using yarns is that—except for bulky all-wool yarns—there are serious practical limitations with yarn rugs. Remember that rugs are meant to be walked on, which creates abrasion on the surface of the rug. Synthetic yarns will pill and wear through quickly with heavy foot traffic, so if you want to use synthetic (and blends with wool or cotton) use your rug lightly—as a bedside rug on top of carpeting for example.

Don't be fooled by synthetic yarns labeled as "rug yarn." They are no more suited for heavy wear than any other synthetic. You may come across vintage knitted rug directions, published by yarn and thread companies that specify rug yarn, but the rug yarns of the 40's and 50's were quite different than the yarns for sale today. The vintage yarns were extraordinarily bulky—what today would be called super-bulky—and they were 100% cotton or 100% wool. Those yarns were well suited to rugs, and if you are lucky enough to stumble on a cache of them, don't let them go.

You can however use multiple strands together to create bulk in a yarn rug, as noted above, or you can create your own heavier yarn by using two or more strands of yarn and chaining them with a crochet hook (chain stitches). The chained yarn is then used directly for the knitting. Just as an example of what it takes to get a rug yarn as bulky as one of the vintage yarns, it took 5 strands of "Peaches and Cream" brand cotton yarn, crocheted into a chain (size K hook) to approximate the same weight and bulk as the old cotton rug yarn.

That same sort of chaining together multiple yarns can also be used to prepare a rug yarn combining wool roving and wool yarn of about the same weights. Wool, of course, is the queen of rug making yarns for its durability, resistance to moisture and warmth. The Halcyon Yarn Company makes a wool rug yarn of fine quality. It is sized for hooked and punched rugs instead of knitting and requires two strands to knit a durable rug.

In recent years, there has been a resurgence of interest in felting wool at home and the felting process creates rugs that are much more durable than unfelted yarn rugs and will compensate in large part for the use of light weight yarns in a rug. Some yarns are very cooperative and will felt in use, but others have to be encouraged a little

There are some excellent felting references available these days—some even specific to felting knitted items, so I'd refer you to those for more techniques and refinements. Felting really does make yarn knitted rugs a practical option, but I still wouldn't use them in high traffic areas or as a scuff mat.

Some recent books and magazine articles have published directions for knitted "rugs" that are simply sweater or afghan patterns laid on the floor. These are utterly impractical and will not hold up to wear. They are simply afghans laid on the floor (and sometimes backed with cotton fabric in an attempt to compensate for their light weight). Knitted rugs must be made with sufficient body that they will not bunch up or "crawl" around the floor.

# PART II:

# KNITTED RAG RUG HANDBOOK

## TOOLS FOR KNITTING RAG RUGS

### Knitting Needles

As in any endeavor, having the right tools will make rug knitting much more efficient and pleasant. The knitting needles themselves are the most important. Size 15 (10mm) knitting needles, 14 inches long are used for most rug making. The needles should be so smooth as to feel slick and have a long taper at the point. My favorites are the metal/ceramic Susan Bates "*Silkon*" brand which are widely available at needlework and yarn shops. They are a little more expensive than the plastic needles but worth every penny since their surface finish is so slick and smooth. If you are using a set of plastic or wooden needles, they may have a rough spot or two on the surface. That roughness will grab on to the fabric strip and make your knitting a more frustrating process. Fabric strip naturally has a lot more friction than yarns so you'll want to smooth your needles as much as possible. Use a 200 grit wet/dry sandpaper or the smoothest side of an emery board to sand down any rough or raised places on the needles.

If you're using a set of needles with a metallic finish you'll notice that the needles feel a little rough. That can be minimized by keeping your hands moisturized and sliding them along the needles occasionally. Just use a very light lotion on your hands and rub it in well. Your hands shouldn't feel greasy, just soft. Slide the tips of your fingers up and down the length of each needle every few rows when the fabric doesn't want to glide along easily.

I have several pairs of size 15 needles since I never seem to have just one rug project going at a time. For rugs knitted in a single section, circular needles are used and I haven't seen my favorite needles made circular yet, so you can use any size 15 circular needles. But one of the interesting challenges in being a rug maker is that often just the right tool isn't commercially available and you have to make it yourself. Here's what I did to modify a pair of the "*Silkon*" needles to make them circular. First, the end caps have to be knocked off. They are on tight so it takes some muscle and pounding. I secured the needles in a vise and used a small board as if it were a blunt chisel so as not to scratch or dent the finish on the needles.

Once the end caps were off, the problem became what to use for the connecting piece between the two needles. Clear plastic tubing

## *Making Your Own Equipment*

*One of the challenges of rug making is that the proper equipment is not available and so you have to make your own. Below are two examples.*

*You can make your own, very long, circular knitting needles using hollow knitting needles and clear plastic tubing. The end caps are removed from the needles and the tubing is glued inside. The transition is smoothed with electricans tape.*

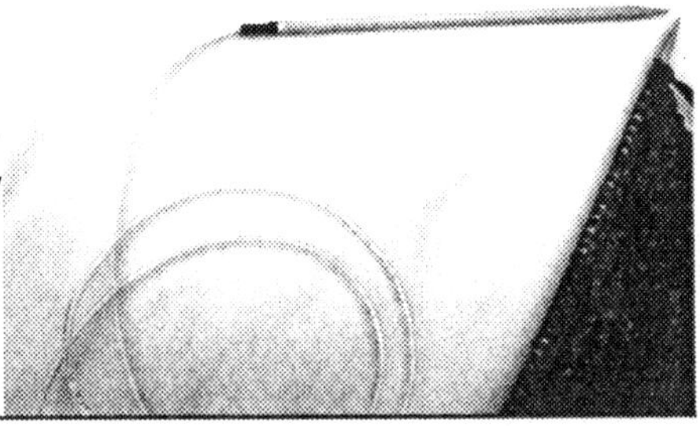

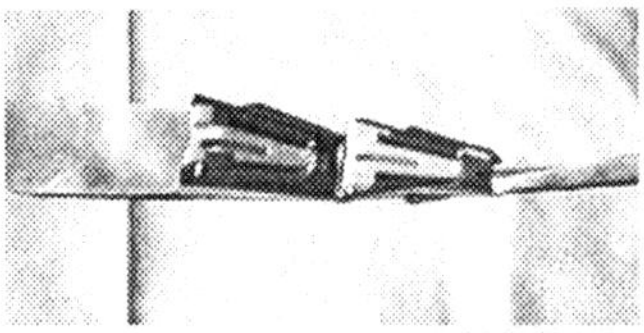

*Double-folding fabric strip is the best way to insure that your rugs are of professional quality. Two bias-tape folders are used in sequence to double-fold strip, and basic equipment makes the folding even easier.*

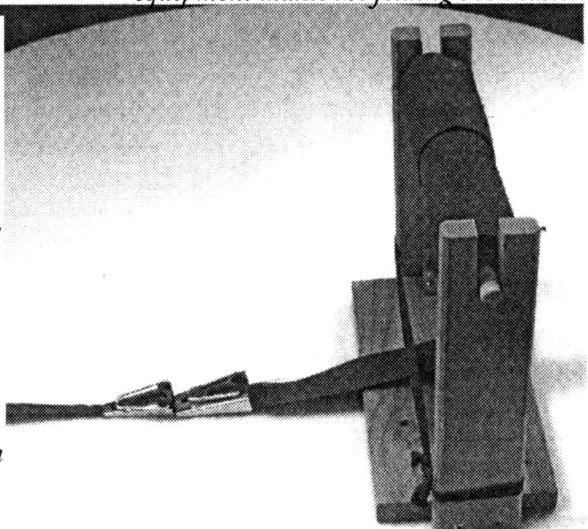

*At right is a basic arrangement for folding. A small wooden stand is constructed to hold a dowel. Fabric strip is rolled ont the dowel as it is joined.*

*For folding, the strip is pulled from the stand through the pair of bias tape folders. Note that around the base of the wooden stand is a section of cord. The cord acts as a thread guide to make sure that the strip comes off of the dowel at the base level, feeding straight through the folders. See the text for a more complete discussion of using bias tape folders.*

of ¼-inch diameter is sold in hardware stores and will fit inside the needles. Cut it to the length that you want for the circular needle plus about six inches to go inside the hollow shafts of the needles. Slit the end of the plastic tube and fill it with hot glue from a glue gun. Immediately slide the tube into the hollow of the needle coating the tube with more hot glue as you go. If you get too much glue on the tube, just scrape it off after it has cooled. To smooth the levels between the ends of the needles and the tubing, wrap with a smooth flexible tape like electrical tape. Because there are occasions that knitting works best along the length of the rug, I've got one pair that is six feet long of these homemade circular needles. Most of the time though a pair three feet long will work though.

**Lacing needles**

These are long needles with a large eye used to lace the tag ends of fabric strip back into the rug. They can be hard to find. Some are sold as "bulky yarn" needles or "weaving" needles. You don't need any particular brand or composition, any needle with a blunt tip and an eye large enough for fabric strip will work fine. Lacing needles can be plastic or metal and any size between two and six inches in length. If you have a large tapestry needle in your sewing basket, check to see if the eye is large enough for your fabric strip. If you just can't find a lacing needle, use a small safety pin on the end of the fabric strip instead. Also, the "pinching" type of bodkin can be used for lacing with heavy or bulky fabrics that won't fit a needle.

**Cutting tools**

If you like the look and feel of torn fabric strips for your rugs, all you need is a pair of sharp sewing scissors. However, if you want to make the more professional-looking rugs with double-folded strip, you'll need equipment to cut a lot of strip efficiently. A rotary cutter and mat are the most flexible for that process. Get the largest size mat you can afford and a good clear plastic cutting guide to fit it. If you fold the fabric neatly into layers, you can cut a 5-yard strip of calico or 3-yard strip of a single knit in a single pass. Even a whole sheet can be cut if it is arranged carefully.

**Basic Sewing Tools**

A sewing machine is useful in joining fabric sections or strips, making the whole process much faster than hand sewing. A yardstick or measuring tape comes in handy to keep track of gauge and the size of your work. A box, basket or plastic bin to hold the rolls of fabric strip while you work is a sanity saver—otherwise the rolls of strip will wander all over entertaining your pets, but not doing you much good.

**Folding Tools**

If you decide to make rugs as a business or to enter in a fair or contest, you'll want to double-fold your cotton strips. This process is made much easier with a pair of bias tape folders used in sequence. The folders need to be of the style that has a flat profile, such as the "Clover" brand. For fabric strip cut 1½ inches wide, you'll need one folder 25 mm size (1 inch) and a second folder 12 mm size (½ inch). The use of the folders is illustrated in the section on fabric preparation.

## FABRICS AND FABRIC PREPARATION

Almost any fabric can be used for knitted rugs, but different fabrics are prepared for knitting in different ways. While you're learning about knitting rugs, I'd suggest that you stick to one type of fabric until you are confident with it. As a general rule, you shouldn't mix different basic types of fabrics in the same rug because they will wear at different rates. For example, cotton knits will wear out much more quickly than woven cottons such as calico or broadcloth, and the rug will look shabby before its time. Similarly, wool fabrics and cotton fabrics need to be handled differently in laundering, so they shouldn't be used in the same rug.

This chapter describes the standard preparation for various types of fabric, but there are other techniques used only for one knitted variation. You'll find those directions in the chapter with the rug in which they are used. With each type of fabric I'm including a seat-of-the-pants fabric consumption estimate for the garter stitch. These are the general fabric guidelines that I've used for years, but note that your actual usage will probably be different. Your knitting touch is likely to be different than mine and if you use alternate stitches, you'll have some left over since some of the lighter stitches don't eat as much fabric as the garter stitch does.

### Light Woven Cottons (Calico, Broadcloth, etc.)

Woven cotton or cotton-blend fabrics (calico, broadcloth, shirtings, etc.) make excellent and durable knitted rugs. These are the traditional fabrics and widely available. Sewing leftovers, old sheets and light cotton clothing are good sources for rug fabrics. Just make sure that the fabrics are tightly woven (have a thread count of 150 threads per inch or more). Otherwise, the fabrics won't tear easily and the rug will wear out more quickly.

Selecting cottons for rug making can be confusing since some fabrics will appear quite differently as yardage than they do in a finished rug. Remember that a rug will usually be seen at a distance of several feet, so stand back from a fabric to note how it appears.

With a little practice you'll recognize good prints for rug making, but here is a general guide as you get started:

- Solid colors will accent the texture of a knitted rug;
- Small closely spaced prints, like tiny florals will blend to an overall impression of a single color;
- Large all-over prints (like tropical florals) will give a general impression of tone (bright, dark, etc.) rather than of a particular color;
- Large widely spaced prints will create a speckled appearance in the rug;
- Watercolor prints will created a blended impression of tone and color;
- Plaids will disguise the texture of the knitting and give only a general impression of color.

Rug making is a way to solve those fabric mistakes that happen sometimes, since even large garish prints or designs will disappear in the rug, leaving only a general impression of the colors of the fabric in the finished rug.

Be warned, however, that if you're one of those people who take up rug making with the idea of finally using up that huge fabric "stash," that it has never happened yet. Once you start working with rugs, you'll be even more susceptible to the sale table at the fabric store. The prints that wouldn't have gotten a second glance before—no matter how cheap they were—are now going to be awfully tempting. You'll be able to see that the stuff that would be terrible for sewing would be just perfect for a rug.

**Fabric consumption.** For 1½-inch strips double-folded, allow 2 yards of 44-45 inch fabric for each square foot of rug. For 1-inch strips used unfolded, allow 1½ yards of 44-45 inch fabric for each square foot.

Woven cotton fabrics can be torn or cut into strips for rug making. Tearing strips from light cottons is the quickest method by far. Pre-wash new fabrics before tearing to remove any sizing and soften the fabric. Rugs made with torn strips have a more informal appearance than those made with cut and double-folded strip, but the time saved in preparation is important if you are making rugs for use around the house. Some people even prefer the look of torn strips as more old-fashioned or softer. This is purely a personal choice.

Strips should be torn one inch wide for rugs and ¾ inch wide for light projects like table runners. Make sure to pull off the loose threads from each piece as soon as it is torn to minimize tangling. You can tear the strips in one continuous process by sewing the yardage into an offset tube or you can tear the strips individually and sew them together using the *overlapping bias joint.* The latter method allows you to mix many different fabrics in sequence if you want blocks of color. Keep in mind that some fabrics shed a lot of lint when they are torn into strips. Ideally, strips should be torn outdoors so you don't have to clean it up or breathe it in.

Knitted rugs and other projects look the neatest when the cotton fabric is double-folded to hide the raw edges. This is *the way* to get a professional-looking rug and a smooth surface texture. It does take more time than tearing strips, but the final product is quite superior. For the folding procedure, see the section titled "Folding Fabric Strips" below.

**Single-knit Fabrics**

The easiest fabrics for beginners to handle are single-knits, whether cotton or synthetic (T-shirt fabric or polyester knits). Most of these fabrics have a natural curl when they are cut into strips which makes the fabric preparation very easy and gives the rug a finished look without much work. (In selecting knit fabrics, look at the cut end on the bolt. If it is already trying to curl, you know you have a great fabric to knit with.) Knitting rugs with single-knit fabric is similar to knitting with yarn and the beginner will find the transition to fabric is easily made.

When using knit fabrics, always test for the direction of the "curl". Most T-shirt fabrics are can be cut along the length of the goods (parallel to the selvage) or across the width of the fabric. Interestingly, the direction of cutting determines which side of the fabric will show when it curls up. Usually, knits cut width-wise will show the back of the fabric and knits cut lengthwise will show the front side. Cut a short test strip one inch wide. Stretch it gently to see if the edges will curl under and which side of the fabric shows. If it creates the effect you want, go ahead and cut all of your strips that way. If it doesn't, cut the other direction.

*Single knit fabrics will generally curl in opposite directions when cut with the lengthwise grain and the cross grain of the fabric. To have the "right" side of the fabric show, cut parallel to the selvage edge. To have the back side show, cut across the grain.*

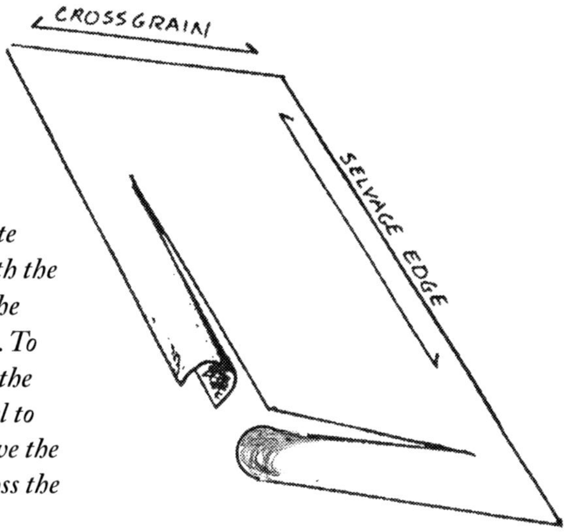


Occasionally single knits will only curl in one direction, so do a test cut both ways. (Some knit fabrics are heavily sized when they are new and may not curl at all until they are washed. If it won't curl at all, it is handled like a double-knit.)

Single knits can be cut as individual strips with scissors or a rotary cutter. They can also be sewn into an offset tube like the woven cottons and *cut* into a continuous strip—don't try to tear knits.

If you have cut the strips individually, join them end to end sewing the bias joint at right angles so that the seams are hidden. That will give the smoothest appearance in the rug. After they are stitched together, pull on the fabric strip firmly to make the strip curl up and hide the raw edges. If you have an ultra-modern décor, look for single knits with a shiny or metallic finish since they make extraordinarily eye-catching rugs.

**Fabric consumption.** Cotton T-shirt knits usually come in 60-inch width, so for each square foot of rug allow one yard of fabric cut into 1-inch strips. If the fabric you are using is of a different width, adjust the fabric allowance accordingly.

### Heavier and Lighter Knit Fabrics

Some sweatshirt knits, velours and velveteens will also curl beautifully for knitting. These fabrics should be cut slightly narrower as a rule, but test a strip. With the heavier knits you will have to pull on the strip harder to get the curl to stay.

Very light knits can also be used for knitting—for example some sheer drapery fabric. These should also be cut as individual strips and you'll want to try a test cut for the direction of the curl and the width you want to handle. Sometimes light knits need to be cut up to 2 inches wide, but I've found 1½ inches works most often. These very light fabrics can be surprisingly durable in a rug, but don't plan to use them in a high traffic area since they will skid around and bunch up. Ideally they should be used only over a carpet.

**Fabric consumption.** Heavier knits in a 60-inch width will require about ¾ yard per square foot of rug. Light knits will vary, but may need up to 1½ yards of fabric per square foot of finished rug.

### Double-knit Fabrics

Double-knit fabrics don't curl naturally and have to be handled like woven fabrics. The strips are cut individually and joined with the overlapping bias joint. These fabrics won't fold in double-folders, so don't bother with that. In general double-knits should be cut one inch wide, but the heavier ones (and textured ones) work best at ¾ inches or even ½ inch.

The vintage polyester double-knits are often extremely durable and fade resistant so they do have their adherents. Other folks swear by rugs made with double-knits since they finally have something they can do just to use up the stuff, or recycle old clothing.

Fabric consumption. Double knits 60 inches wide will require about ¾ yard for each square foot of rug. If the fabrics are narrower or pretty light weight, allow 1 to 1¼ yards for each square foot.

### Wool Fabrics

Wool fabric strip can be one of the most difficult to handle in knitting because of its bulk and is not recommended for the beginner. There are too many types of wool to list individually, but in general, light weight woolens are the easiest. These are cut on the straight grain of the fabric, ¾ inches wide, and joined using an overlapping bias joint. Sewing such small seams is aggravating, so it is easier to handle them in a modified joint illustrated in the section on joining rug strips below. Begin with a length of wool 3 to 12 inches wide. Set up an overlapping bias joint with the two ends off-set ¾ of an inch. Sew the bias seam with two closely spaced lines of stitching and clip off the excess of the corners. Then cut the wool in the tube style to the ¾ inch width, trying to keep the cuts as even as possible.

Heavy woolens from coats or blankets can be cut in similar fashion to a ½ inch width.

**Polar Fleece**

Fleece fabrics are a relatively new addition to the rug making world and they present unique characteristics. Fleece is usually 100% polyester applied on a knit fabric base and is a wonderful insulator against cold floors. It is machine washable (cool) and dryable (cool) and is not subject to disintegration from a moist environment. Fleece is easy for a beginner to handle in knitting since it has some stretch, but has one very big drawback when used for rugs. Fleece rugs are extremely slippery and should *never* be used directly on smooth floors. Instead, use them over carpeting or with a non-skid rug backing underneath. Even with a non-skid backing, fleece rugs can be unpredictable so don't use them in bathrooms or heavy traffic areas.

Because fleece fabrics are so heavy, it is best to prepare fleece by cutting a single piece in a spiral to avoid seams joining individual strips. Garment weight fleece is best for knitting and is cut in one-inch strips. Blanket weight fleece is a little harder to handle, but can be cut in ¾-inch strips. Allow one yard of 60-inch fleece fabric for each square foot of the finished rug. Fleece strips don't ravel so they are not prefolded, but just used as-is for knitting.

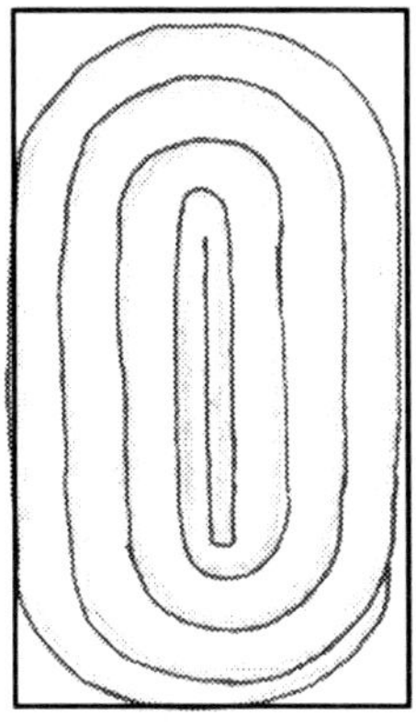

*Fleece fabrics are cut in a continuous spiral to minimize seams. Select a piece of fabric one to two yards in length. Round off the corners. Then cut a one-inch strip continuously from the outside edge to the center. Generally, the innermost two-inch width is discarded.*

### Novelty Fabrics

Specialty fabrics can be used to achieve dramatic effects in knitted rugs. Metallics, silks, linens, and such work well in knitted projects. Don't be afraid to experiment. The only practical consideration when using specialty fabrics is washability. If the rug will be subject to heavy soil, make sure to test wash all fabrics before using them. Shiny fabrics should be double-folded to accent their appearance. As a general rule, woven novelty fabrics can be handled like woven cottons and knitted novelties like cotton knit fabric. To estimate the fabric consumption for novelty fabrics, find a fabric above that is of about the same weight.

### Denim, Canvas and Other Heavy Cotton Fabrics

Heavy cotton fabrics can be used for knitted rugs but are not very cooperative. These fabrics should probably be saved for shaggy knitted rugs or other varieties of rugs that are more suited to the weight of these fabrics. But heavy fabrics can be knitted if you don't mind the work. Pre-wash these fabrics to soften them. Strips are cut ½- to ¾-inches wide, always on the bias (diagonal) because extra give is needed to knit with these fabrics. Rugs made with these fabrics will have a 'rustic' look because it is impossible to fold the raw edges under. In use, these rugs will develop a softer texture, especially after laundering. Use the overlapping bias joint to join strips of these heavy fabrics if they are cut from recycled clothing. Use the modified overlapping bias joint if you are cutting pieces of any significant size.

# CARING FOR KNITTED RAG RUGS

I know it seems odd to have a section on caring for rugs just after the fabric selection discussion, but when selecting your fabrics keep in mind that the fabric you choose will determine how you clean the finished rug. These days most homemakers want easy-care accessories for the home. Knitted rugs are no exception. So long as you use washable fabrics in making your rug, it will be washable.

Hotpads, placemats, chairpads and rugs up to 36 inches across can all be machine washed—if you make them from washable fabrics. (Use the gentle cycle, a mild detergent and no bleach.) Washing is usually not required more than once every few months for knitted rugs that receive basic care. The rugs should be shaken out regularly and vacuumed using the suction-only attachment (usually labeled the upholstery tool).

Small projects can machine washed and dried in any home dryer. Rugs should not be dried in the dryer since they become too heavy when wet for most home machines. Instead, lay the damp rug flat to dry, out of direct sunlight. Large rugs may be draped over a clothesline, railing or banister for preliminary drying, but when they are still slightly damp, they should be laid flat to finish. Shape the rug for the last part of its drying.

## Cleaning Large Rugs

To clean rugs that are too large for a washing machine, a carpet cleaning machine is recommended. Machines which spray water on the rug and then suck it out are the best. Never use a machine with rotating brushes. Always clean both sides of the knitted rug. Do not use the aerosol spray rug cleaners on knitted rugs. They can damage the fabrics.

## Storing Knitted Rugs

If you need to store your knitted rug for any length of time, it should be *rolled up*, not folded. Roll the rug with the front side in the center, if like shaggy knitted rugs, it has a distinct front and back. Do not use mothballs with stored rugs. Instead, wrap the rug in a cotton sheet and store in a sealed container. Always make sure that the rug is clean and completely dry before storing.

## CUTTING AND TEARING FABRIC STRIPS

Woven cotton fabrics can be cut or torn to make strips for rugs. If you do not want to fold the strip for your rug, it is best to tear the fabric into strips after pre-washing it to remove the sizing. (Old clothing has already been washed, so it is ready to tear.) Just clip the edge of the fabric an inch or two down and hold the two sections apart and pull. The fabric should tear along a straight thread. If it doesn't, the fabric is either too worn to use for rugs or is too loosely woven to tear. After tearing remove any loose threads that cling to the strip.

Some "homespun" types of fabrics are woven with a heavier cotton thread and some of them will tear and fold themselves if they are handled just right. Prewash the fabric. Make a tear for the first rug strip and if the edge of the strip wants to turn over, you're in luck. Make the next tear from the opposite end of the fabric to get the edges turning over to the same side. Finish tearing the strip alternating the end of the fabric from which the strip is torn each time.

Cotton knit fabrics have to be cut since they won't tear cleanly. Before cutting, test for the direction of the curl in the fabric. Usually with single-knit fabrics, a lengthwise cut will curl up into a tube which shows the "right side" of the fabric, and cutting along the width will show the "wrong side" or back of the fabric. If you made the T-shirt project in Chapter 1, you were cutting in a spiral across the fabric so that the back of the fabric curled to the outside of the strip. If you want to use T-shirts for rugs and have the "right side" show, cut the shirt lengthwise (from hem to shoulder) and then join the strips using the regular bias joint. That will hide the seams in the finished strip when it curls up.

If you want to double-fold woven cotton fabric strip, the fabric should not be pre-washed before cutting since a little sizing helps the strip glide more smoothly through the folders. Strip should always be cut (not torn) if it is going to be folded.

Fabric strips can be cut using a good, sharp pair of scissors with a yardstick as a guide. I recommend the Fiskars brand of scissors with their small sharpener, since it is easy to keep a good edge on the blades. If you're going to be doing a lot of cutting, the investment in a good cutting mat, cutting guide and roller knife is worthwhile. Purchase the largest cutting mat that you can afford and make sure it is a brand of mat that is "self-healing" since you will be using the same surface over and over. Yard goods can be folded to several layers and cut with a single pass of a roller knife. It does take a little practice to get good with the tools, so ask at the sewing store or ask a quilting friend to show you the best way to hold the guide and the knife.

When you have all of your strip cut, you're ready to join them into a continuous length for rug making. Match the type of strip that you want to use with the joining method.

*Some fabrics will cooperate with being torn into strips. The top two samples are of a "homespun" type of cotton fabric, which, when torn from alternating ends, curls its own edges in and folds without any added effort.*

*The sample at the bottom is of a coton fabric with a thread count too low to tear cleanly. Notice how the fabric has fractured and the edges are very loose.*

# JOINING STRIPS FOR RUG MAKING

## The Overlapping Bias Joint

Use this joining with unfolded strips. The diagonal seam will spread the bulk of the fabric out so that it doesn't form a bump in the rug. See Chapter 2 for a diagram of this joining. When you want to use wool fabrics or heavier cotton fabrics for knitting a *modified* overlapping bias joint is used. This procedure is the most efficient for any type of strip that has to be cut less than one inch wide.

## The Regular Bias Joint

This joining is used with strip that will be folded or curled into a tube. In sewing this joint the "right sides" of the fabric are placed together so that the seam is on the "wrong side" of the fabric. The seam is hidden entirely within the strip when the strip is folded (woven cottons) or curled (single-knit fabrics) and is nearly invisible in the finished rug. See the illustration of how to make this joint.

## No-Sew Ways to Add Strip or Change Colors

Because there are folks who don't sew and those like myself who find themselves outdoors making rugs, it is useful to know how to add strip or change colors of strip when a sewing machine isn't handy. There are at least eight different slit-and-loop methods of splicing fabric strip, but there is only one—**the bow tie joint**—that doesn't result in a noticeably thick and lumpy knot, so that is the only one I recommend for making knitted rugs. In the chapter on shaggy rugs is a variation of the "bow tie joint" to make a shaggy rug, but for general knitting purposes, the bow tie joint can be used for regular knitted ugs too. Using the bow tie joint is not as efficient as the joints made on sewing machines, but are good because they can be done anywhere using just a small pair of scissors.

Cut or tear the fabric strips for the rug one to 1½ inches wide—choose one width for the entire rug. You'll want the strips to be as long as you can get from the piece of fabric that you are using. At both ends of each strip clip a tiny slit one inch or a little more from the end. The slit should be as small as possible—just large enough for another

## *The Regular Bias Joint*

*Use for all fabrics that will be folded including single knits*

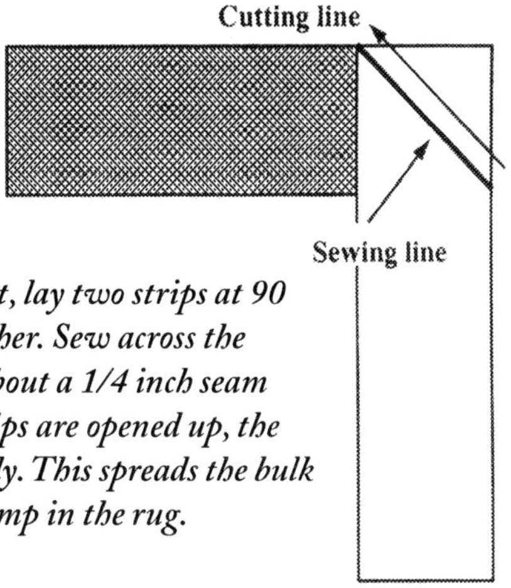


*To make the regular bias joint, lay two strips at 90 degrees with right sides together. Sew across the corner and clip off, leaving about a 1/4 inch seam allowance. When the two strips are opened up, the seam should appear diagonally. This spreads the bulk of the seam and prevents a lump in the rug.*

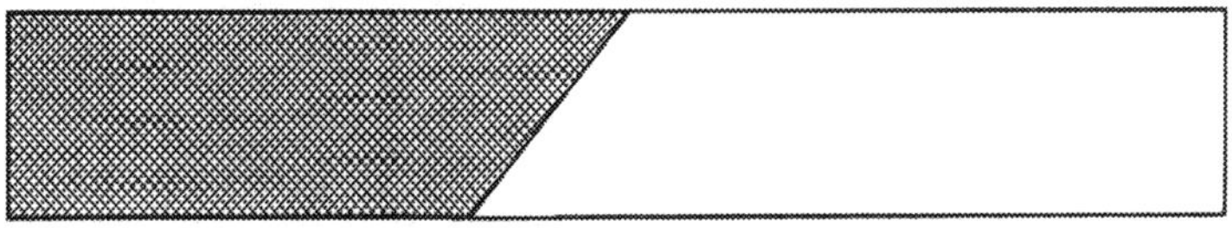

## *The Modified Overlapping Bias Joint*

*for use with wool and other heavy fabrics used unfolded*

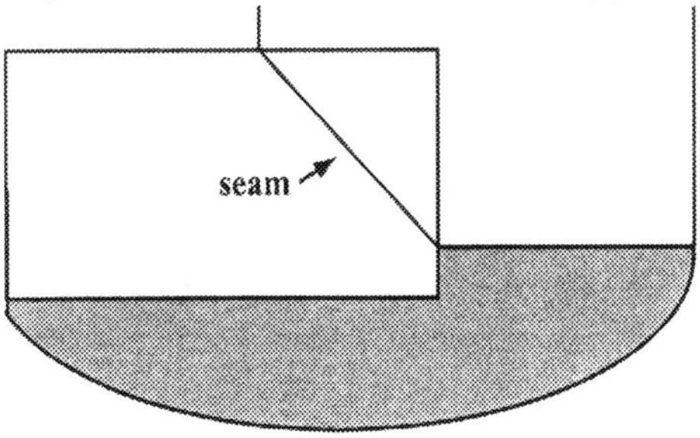


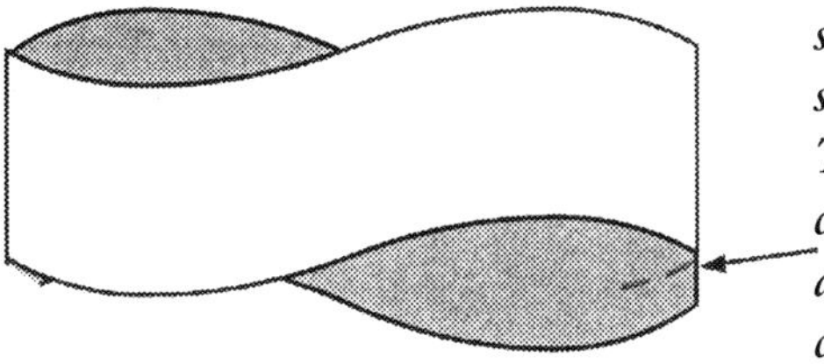

*Cut the fabric into a section about 12 inches wide and overlap the ends so that they are offset by the width of the strip. The overlap needs to be deep enough to allow for the diagonal seam shown. Clip the seam allowance on both sides to about 1/4 inch. Then cut the strips in a continous spiral. Begin at one of the offset corners.*

### *The "Bow Tie" Joint for General Rug Making*

***(for the variation of this joint used only in shaggy rugs, see Chapter 4)***

***Short strips of lightweight woven or knit fabrics can be joined without sewing using this joint. Begin by making a small slit in the end of each strip to be joined. The slit should be about one inch from the end of the strip, and only just large enough to allow the strip to pass through. The knitting needle in the photo is just to illustrate the size of the slits.***

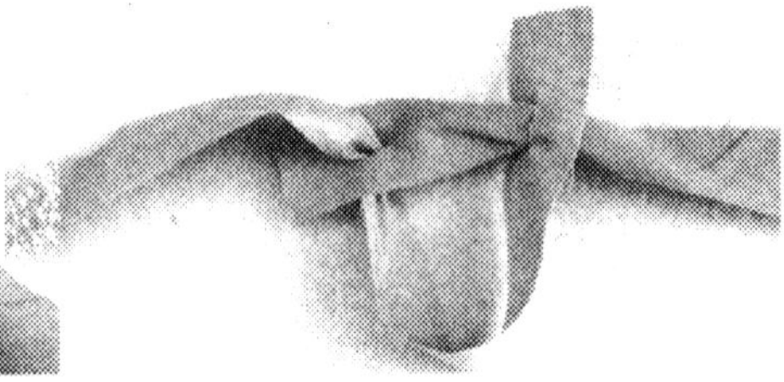

***Begin by passing the strip that is ending through the slit in the fabric that is being added on (left). Then pass the other end of the new fabric through the slit in the older strip (right).***

***Pull lightly on the two strips to tighten the joint. The "bow tie" is formed as the strip ends come together (right).***

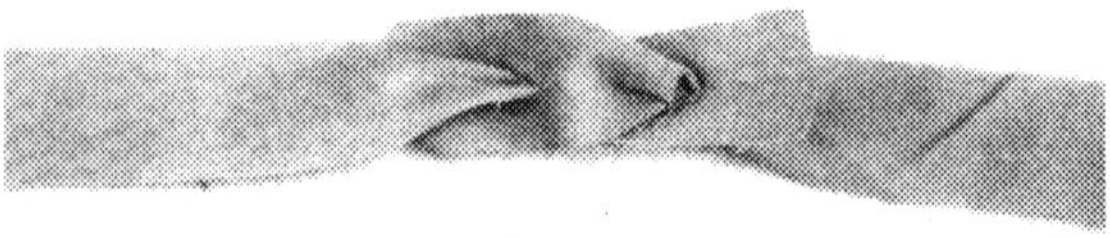

***Snug the joint, making sure that the strip ends lay close to the opposite strip, and curl around it to form a smooth joining.***

strip to pass through. Because the slit should be small a pair of embroidery scissors or thread nippers is a good tool to use. Make sure that the end of the slit is at least an inch from the end of the fabric strip.

Insert the end of the first strip into the slit in the second strip. Then insert the end of the second strip through the slit in the first strip. (See illustration.) Pull gently to tighten the knot and adjust the strip ends so that they lay flat and curl around the strip forming a bow tie sort of shape. As you knit, try to keep these ends laying flat against the strip. If you find that a corner sticks up from the knitting anyway it can be clipped off—but only if it is a corner. If the whole end sticks up for some reason, it will need to be tucked back into the knitted stitch.

When I'm outdoors and want to change colors, I use an even easier method which I'll call the "**just drop it**" method. This should only be used to switch from one ball of strip to the next—not with short strips. If I run out of strip in the middle of a row, I just stop knitting with the old strip and leave a tail at least 4 inches long hanging loose. Then I pick up the new ball of strip and start knitting with it—also leaving a tail. I proceed with the knitting for several rows (and sometimes the whole piece) and then go back and lace the ends into the work. Cross the two tails just once so that they go around each other. Then thread the tail ends of the strips into a large-eye lacing needle and work them into the knitting for several stitches. Usually, a couple of small hand sewn stitches are all it takes to hold the ends in place and any excess can just be clipped off.

## *The "Just Drop It" Method to Add Strip or Change Colors*

***When you come to the end of a ball of rug strip or want to change colors cleanly, you can just drop the ending strip and begin knitting with a new ball or color. Leave about a 6-inch tail of each of the strips, and continue knitting. To finish off the work, the tails are worked back into the rug as shown.***

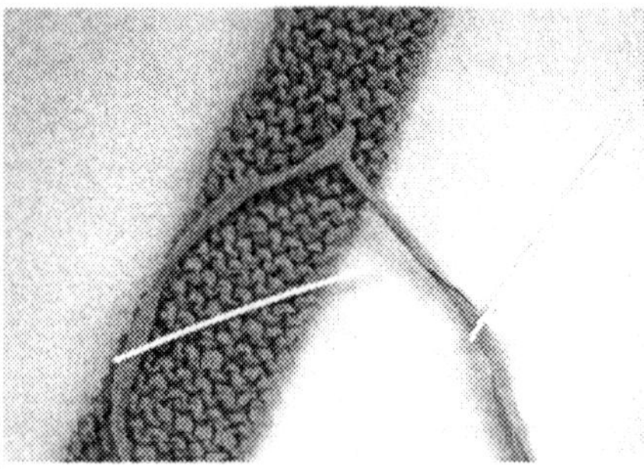

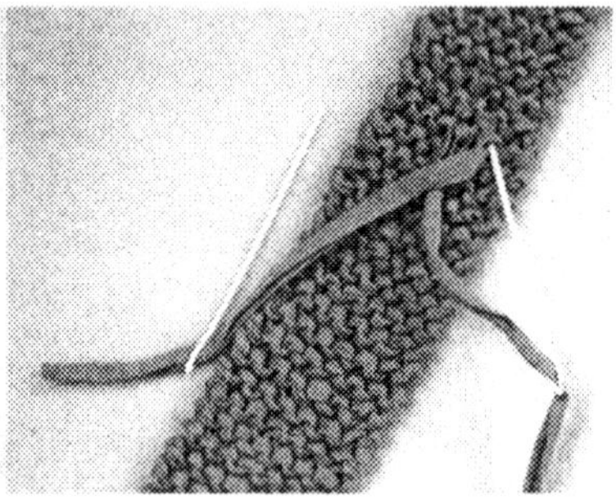

***The two strips are crossed and the end is threaded into a lacing needle (left). Then insert the lacing needle into the stitch on the opposite side (right), and work in under several stitches. Hand sew the strip in place and clip off any ex-***

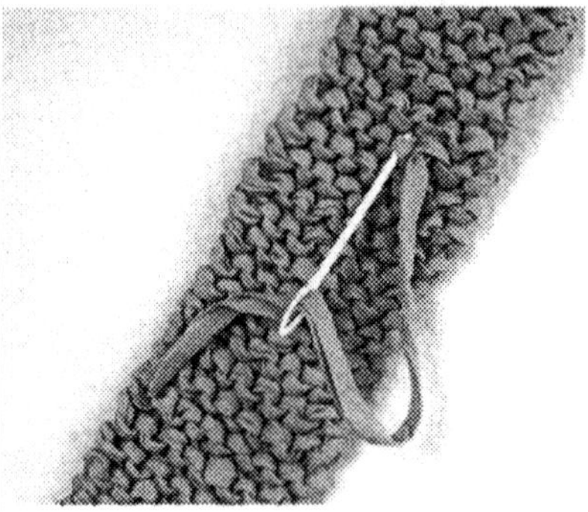

***Repeat the process with the other strip (left). The joining will be nearly invisible in the finished knitting (right).***

***At left, the same procedure is being used to change colors cleanly at the outer edge of a wedge knitted rug. When you drop and add strip at the outer edge, make a loose overhand knot with the pair of strip tails to keep them in place until you are ready to lace them into the knitting.***

# FOLDING STRIPS FOR RUGS

If you want to make professional-looking rugs with woven cotton fabrics, you need to know how to double-fold the strips to hide the raw edges. Particularly if you are intending to sell your rugs, using folded strips will give you the greatest return for your time. The strip for some older rugs was ironed by hand which is quite time-consuming, but it does work. You'll be able to fold strip much more efficiently using a pair of folders.

Do not pre-wash fabrics that you plan to double-fold. For light cottons cut the fabric strip 1½ inches wide straight on the grain of the fabric (parallel to the selvage). Do not include the selvage in the cut strips since it has a different weight than the rest of the fabric. Never cut woven light cottons on the bias (diagonal) since the strip will continue to stretch even after the rug is made and the rug won't hold its shape well.

Cut the strips using scissors or a rotary cutter and mat. Then sew the strips into one continuous length using the regular "bias joint" (see illustration). These strips will be easiest to fold if they are rolled onto a dowel or cardboard tube as they are sewn. The tube from a roll of paper towels works well. Make sure that all of the seams are going the same direction. With print fabrics, it is easy to sew the right sides together, but solid color fabrics are a different story and you have to watch the seams carefully.

The old fashioned-way of double-folding was simply to fold the edges under and then fold the strip in half and iron it by hand. I've seen yards and yards of this rug strip carefully put away for decades and it always amazes me how much labor must have gone into a rug with fabrics prepared this way.

When I first began rug making, I wasn't much more efficient. I would double-fold the fabric strip by hand and roll it into a tight ball. I'd discovered that you really didn't need to iron cotton strips since just heat would set the folds. So the hand rolled balls went into the oven set on "Warm" for a couple of hours. This really only worked well with cotton and blends that were at least 70% cotton.

I knew there had to be a better way and by experimentation found that two bias tape folders used in sequence would double-fold fabric strip. These only work though when the strip to be folded is fed perfectly straight through the folders. If you have a good friend or patient spouse or child, they can handle the feeding operation while you pull the strip through the folders and iron it or roll it up tightly. That works for a little while until your helper goes on strike.

Most of the time a rug maker will need to be able to handle the folding operation single-handedly which means you'll need some modest equipment. As you are starting, the easiest set up is to use a paper towel tube. As you sew the strips together wind them flat (no twists) onto the cardboard tube. When the strips are all rolled up, you'll need a spindle to put the tube onto. In a pinch, a broomstick handle will fit through the tube—just prop the ends of the broom between two kitchen chairs. The roll can be several feet from where you set up the folders. If you think you're going to be doing a lot of rug making, it is worth the time to make yourself a simple wooden stand like the one shown in the illustration. The uprights are cut out to hold a dowel, and the fabric strip can be rolled directly onto the dowel as shown or the dowel can hold a paper towel tube with the fabric strip on it. Just be sure not to twist the strip as you roll it onto the dowel or tube.

Next you'll need to secure the folders so that they don't move. If you're going to iron the strip as it comes out of the folders, this can be done with large safety pins set into an old ironing board cover. A more practical solution is to make a permanent folder-holder on a small piece of wood or paneling. Use a heavy fabric (like a scrap of denim) cut and inch or two wide. Place the smallest folder in position on the board, lay the denim strip across it and thumbtack it to the board (or use a staple gun). The fabric sleeve should be tight enough to keep the folder from moving, and solidly connected to the board so that it won't work loose as you pull the strip through the folders. Then set the larger folder in place and make a sleeve for it just the same way. Don't try to use a single sleeve for both folders since you'll need to be able to remove the folders individually in case of a jam. Your folding board can then be clamped to the ironing board. If you are just going to roll the strip into balls, the board can be clamped to a tabletop or other convenient spot.

Feed the strip from the roll straight through the folders *wrong side up* so that the seam allowances will be hidden within the folded strip. Then pull a length of strip through the folders and iron it or roll it up. If you feel like more tension is needed, set a heavy book or two on top of the strip just before it enters the folders.

Of course, over the years I've designed and built more and more elaborate folding apparatuses and each was at least some improvement in efficiency over the previous models. But the use of two bias tape folders together is still the basis for double-folding. There are all sorts of possibilities if you want to get creative, but complicated folding machinery isn't really necessary even if you plan to go into the rug-making business.

## ALTERNATE STITCH PATTERNS FOR KNITTED RUGS

Most of the rug projects in this book give basic directions specifying the garter stitch. There are however other stitch patterns offering a variety of textures. Not all of these are suited to every type of knitted rug. The stitches for creating shaggy knitted rugs are all in Chapter 4 and the Fabric Stitch or Woven Stitch is described in Chapter 13.

**Garter Stitch (all types of knitted rugs):**
Cast on the desired number of stitches.
Row 1: Slip 1, Knit across
Repeat Row 1 until work reaches the desired length.

**Shingle Pattern (all types except the very center of coiled, bullseye and wedge rugs):**
Cast on an even number of stitches that is not divisible by 4 (e.g. 18. 22, 26, 30, 34, 38, 42, 46, 50)
Row 1: Slip 1, Knit Across
Row 2: Slip 1, Knit across
Row 3: Slip 1, Knit 1, *Purl 2, Knit 2*, repeat * to end of row
Row 4: Slip 1, Purl 1, * Knit 2, Purl 2*, repeat * to end of row.
Repeat rows 1 through 4 in sequence until work reaches the desired length.

## *Alternate Stitch Patterns for Knitted Rag Rugs*

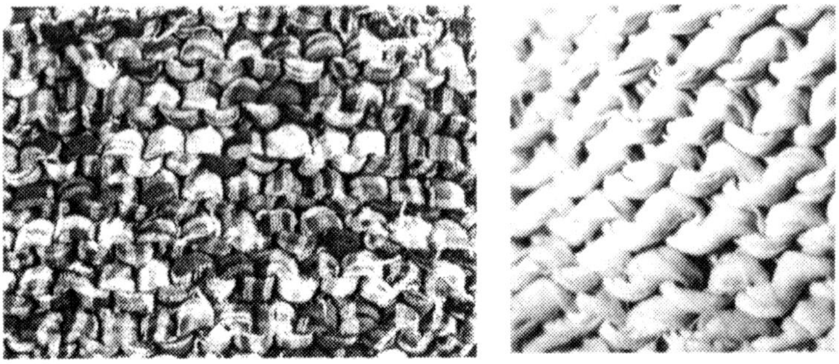

*Above left is the standard garter stitch made with a plaid fabric. Note how the texture is disguised. Above right is the double-sided garter sttich.*

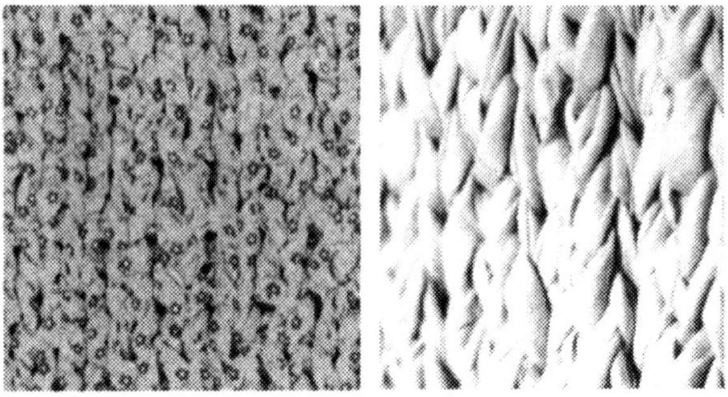

*At the left above is a plain stockinette stitch, Note how its texture is disguised by the use of a small floral print. Next to it is the high density stockinettette stitch.*

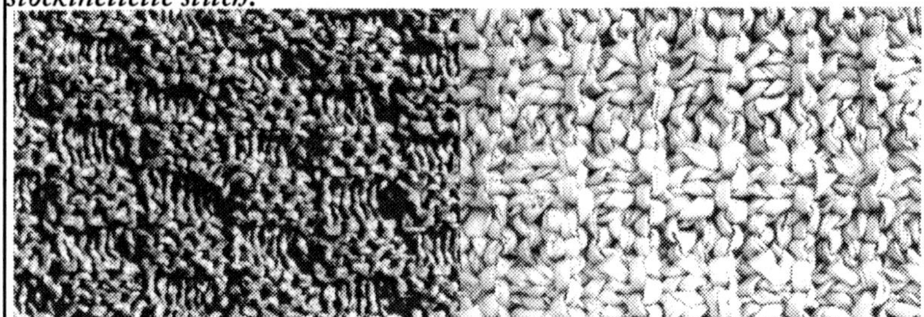

*Above is a side by side comparison of the reversed Checkerboard Stockinette (left) and the Shingle Pattern stitch (right).*

**Double-sided Garter Stitch**
**(strip and block rugs, floor pillows and chairpads):**

The double-sided garter stitch actually creates an open flat tube. It is nearly twice the thickness of the plain garter stitch, and requires 1½ times as much fabric as the plain garter stitch. This type of knitted rug should be used where a thick, spongy rug is desired. It is fully reversible, and can be subjected to very heavy traffic.

Allow 2½ yards of 45" wide cotton fabric per square foot of rug. OR allow 1-1/3 yards of single-knit cotton fabric 60 inches wide for each square foot.

Gauge: 13 stitches = 3 inches
10 rows = 3 inches.

**Directions:**

Cast on an odd number of stitches.
Row 1: Knit across
Row 2: *Knit 1, Slip 1*, repeat * across ending with a Knit 1.
Row 3: *Slip 1, Knit 1*, repeat * across ending with a Slip 1
Repeat rows 2 and 3 until work reaches the desired length. For the final row, knit each stitch across as you cast off.

After several rows you'll be able to pull on the two sides of the work and feel the opening between them. This knitted tube construction makes the double-sided garter stitch ideal for such projects as chairpads or pillows since an inner layer of padding or foam can be inserted before the knitting is completed. This inner pad plumps up the knitting.

To create a knitted rag pillow, decide the width of the pillow and calculate how many stitches you will need to cast on. Add a dozen stitches to the number to accommodate the thickness of the pillow (remember that you need an odd number of total stitches). Follow the basic knitting directions for the double-sided garter but do not knit the final row until you have stuffed the pillow.

To stuff the pillow you will have to open up the knitted tube. To do this, work across the row and pass every other stitch onto a dowel or another knitting needle. Insert a fabric covered pad or pillow form. The padding should be ½" smaller all around than the knitting. Once the pad is inserted, pass the stitches in order from the dowel back onto the knitting needle. Then complete the final row of knitting as you cast off. You can even make a folding floor chair by knitting two of these pillows and lacing them together at one end.

**Stockinette Stitch (strip and block rugs):**
Cast on the desired number of stitches
Row 1: Slip 1, Knit across
Row 2: Slip 1, Purl across
Repeat Rows 1 and 2 until work reaches the desired length.

**Ribbed Stockinette Stitch (strip and block rugs):**
Cast on an even number of stitches
Knit 1, Purl 1* Repeat across and repeat for all rows.
(This stitch replicates the texture of the double-sided raked knitted rug. It is also suited for use with yarns to create a thicker rug.)

**Reversed Checkerboard Stockinette Stitch (strip and block rugs):**
(This stitch forms a springier surface than plain stockinette, but looks fancier than the garter stitch. I developed this pattern to eliminate the need for edging a knitted rug made with stockinette. It was the precursor to the shingle pattern, which has even more body.)
Cast on any number of stitches that is divisible by 8.
Row 1: *Knit 4, Purl 4* and repeat to end of row
Row 2: *Purl 4, Knit 4* and repeat to end of row
Row 3: Repeat Row 1
Row 4: Repeat Row 2
Row 5: Repeat Row 2
Row 6: Repeat Row 1
Row 7: Repeat Row 2
Row 8: Repeat Row 1
To continue: Rows 1 through 8 are repeated until the rug reaches the desired size. Always end the piece by casting off at either Row 4 or Row 8

**High Density Stockinette Stitch (strip and block rugs):**

The high-density Stockinette stitch forms a tighter, harder and more durable rug surface than the plain stockinette stitch. The rug is slightly thicker. It is suitable for rugs that will receive heavy traffic.

Allow 1¾ yards of 45-inch wide woven cottons, cut into 1½-inch strips for each square foot of the rug. Or allow 7/8 yard of 60-inch wide cotton T-shirt fabric, cut into one inch strips for each square foot.

Gauge: 11 stitches = 3 inches
7 rows = 3 inches

**Directions:**

Cast on an odd number of stitches.
Row 1: Knit across
Row 2: *Purl 1, Slip 1*, repeat * across ending with a Purl.
Row 3: *Slip 1, Knit 1*, repeat * across ending with a Knit.
Repeat rows 2 and 3 until the work reaches the desired length. For the last row of the rug strip, knit each stitch across as you cast off.

**Corn-on-the-Cob Stitch (strip and block rugs):**

The corn-on-the-cob stitch presents one of the most interesting textures of any knitted rug. Rows of small raised knobs are alternated in two colors. The corn-on the-cob knitted rug is quite firm—making it very durable.

The corn-on-the-cob stitch is slower to complete than some of the other knitted rug stitches and it uses up more fabric than most. This stitch should be done with purchased fabric yardage, not scrap fabric, so that the stitch pattern covers the entire rug in the same two colors.

Woven cotton fabrics are recommended (calico, broadcloth, etc.), and you will need to buy sufficient fabric of both colors to complete the rug. For each square foot of rug allow one yard of each fabric (two yards total). When choosing your fabrics, remember that this pattern shows best when you use fabrics with a lot of contrast (one light fabric and one dark fabric). Fabric strips should be cut 1½ inches wide and double-folded to hide the raw edges.

Gauge: 6 stitches = 3 inches
12 rows = 3 inches

Be sure to knit a sample piece before you begin the rug. Your knitting will become more even, and the pattern will show better with a little practice.

## *Alternate Stitches for Knitted Rag Rugs*

*(The most interesting ones)*

***The Corn-on-the-Cob stitch makes a showy rug with rows of raised knobs in alternating colors. The most effective use of this stitch is with two contrasting colors of different tones. Single knit fabrics create a smoother texture than woven fabrics with this stitch.***

***The "woven" or "fabric" stitch creates a low profile rug with a woven texture on the front side (at left) and a good imitation of a Berber on the reverse (below). Shown is the stitch done with a single knit cotton fabric in a solid color to emphasize the texture.***

***See Chapter 13 on cross woven rugs for more information about using this stitch.***

**Corn-on-the-Cob Stitch**

**Directions:**

Cast on an even number of stitches with the lighter colored fabric strip.

**Row 1**: Knit across, using the lighter color.

**Row 2**: Use dark color . *Knit 1, Slip 1*, repeat * across row. End with a knit, not a slip.

**Row 3**: Use dark color. *Bring strip to front, Slip 1, take strip to back, Knit 1* Repeat * across row. Note that the knit stitches are all made into the dark stitches on the needle.

**Row 4**: Use light color. *Slip 1, Knit 1 into the back of the stitch* Repeat * across row. Note that all of the knits are made into the light stitches on the needle.

**Row 5**: Use light color. *Knit 1, Bring strip to front, Slip 1, take strip to back* Repeat * across row. Note that all of the knits are made into the light stitches on the needle.

**To continue**: Repeat Rows 2 through 5 in sequence until the work reaches the desired length. Always end the work with Row 5, then knit one row with the dark color and cast off.

Note that the finished rug section will have a small light color border at the beginning of the strip, and a small border of dark knitting at the end. All the strips should be knitted this same way.

As you finish knitting all strips, and are ready to assemble them, align the knitted sections so that the light borders line up together. This also aligns the directions of the stitching so that the finished rug appears as a unit. Because the corn-on-the-cob rug is a thick rug, a border of crochet stitches can be used.

# USING GRAPH PAPER TO ESTIMATE FABRIC CONSUMPTION

In the fabric preparation section above, general guidelines are given for estimating how much fabric it will take to complete a square foot of finished rug. If you are planning a rug of just one fabric, those numbers are pretty straightforward to use. For example, a rectangular rug, three feet wide and five feet long will have 15 square feet in the finished rug. If you make it of 1½ inch woven cotton strip, each square foot will require about two yards of fabric, so for the entire rug you'll want to allow 30 yards of fabric.

But if you plan on using several different fabrics in the same rug—and you want to know how much of each fabric will be needed for your design—the easiest way to find out is to draw the rug to scale using graph paper. Since I'm used to the English system of measurements, I typically use a ¼-inch grid graph paper where each square is equal to four inches. Three squares is equal to one foot and nine squares are equal to one *square* foot. The illustration is shown using that scale. (If you are more familiar with metric measures, a scale based on 10 squares to the meter is easier.)

Simply draw your rug to scale on the graph paper—using colored pencils to show colors if you like. Then count the squares that each color covers. The number of squares divided by 9 will give you how many square feet of each color will be in the rug. Then multiply the number of square feet by the yardage allowance for the type of fabric you plan on using.

These allowance figures are a little generous, since I've found that it is always better to allow for the "oops" factor. The most commonly used fabrics are:

- Light woven cotton fabrics 44 inches wide, cut into strips 1½ inches wide, will take about two yards per square foot of rug;
- Light woven cotton fabrics 44 inches wide, cut or torn into strips one inch wide, will take about 1½ yards per square foot of rug; and
- Light cotton single knit fabric 60 inches wide, cut into strips one inch wide, will take about one yard per square foot of rug.

## *Estimating Fabric Requirements for a Knitted Rug Using Graph Paper*

In order to calculate how much fabric of each color you will need for a rug, you have to determine how many square feet of knitting will be done with each color. Use a sheet of graph paper with squares about ¼ inch in size. Each square will be equal to four inches, so three squares will be one foot long and nine squares will be equal to one square foot.

Using colored pencils, draw your rug design to scale. For a practice example, use the 40" X 48" rectangular rug on the following page. It is planned for eight-inch knitted strips for the center and the border, using three different fabrics. To estimate the yards of fabric needed, count the squares taken up by each fabric in the drawing.

- *Fabric for the border*: takes 72 squares on the graph paper, divided by 9 squares per square foot equals 8 square feet of this fabric knitted to make the rug.
- *Fabric for two outer knitted strips*: takes 32 squares, divided by 9 equals 3-1/2 square feet of this fabric knitted.
- *Fabric for the center strip*: takes up 16 squares on the paper, divided by 9 equals 1-3/4 yards of this fabric knitted.

Now you can consult the stitch and type of fabric to see how many yards of fabric that it will take to knit one square foot and multiply to get the yardage needed to complete your project. For this example, let us assume that the fabric will be a light woven cotton, cut into 1½ inch strips. It takes two yards of these fabrics to knit one square foot. Multiplying the square feet calculated above, the three fabrics will require 16, 7 and 3½ yards respectively.

Estimating yardage for odd shapes can be done in the same manner. Around curves, there will be partial squares of the graph paper covered by your design. If the design covers half or more of the block, count it as a full block. If the design covers less than half of the block, don't count it in the total. Use the sketches of the round and oval rugs on the opposite page to practice counting squares of each color and calculating how many square feet of each fabric will be knitted into the rug.

***Estimating Fabric Consumption Using Graph Paper***

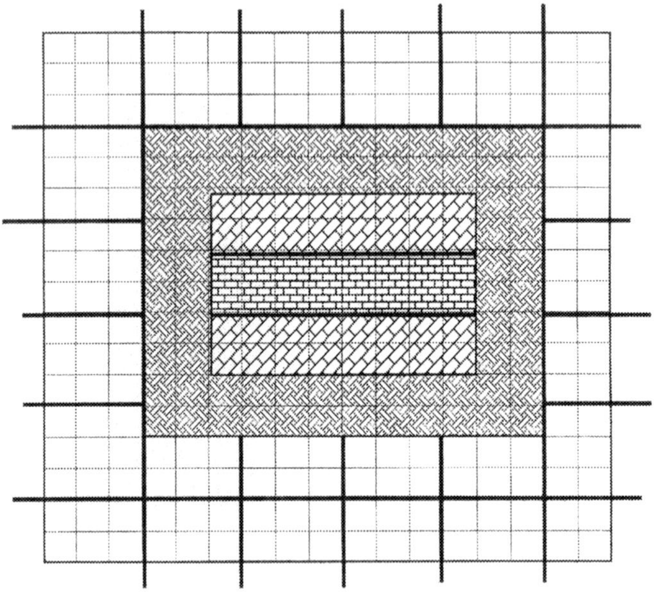

*Above a 40" X 48" Rectangle planned for 8-inch strips.*
*Below a 32" round and 30" X 68" oval.*

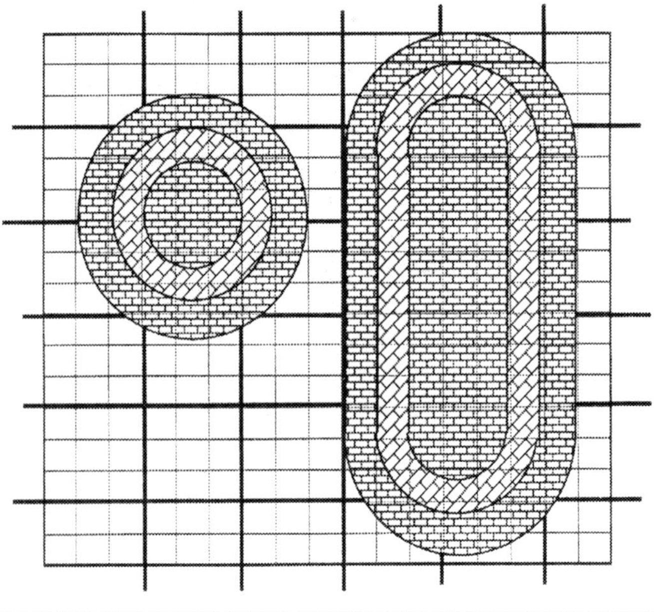

# LACING TOGETHER RUG SECTIONS

The order of lacing together rug sections depends on the type of rug construction that you are using.

- For "strip" rugs: lace the rug sections together after all of the pieces have been knitted.
- For "block" (except hexagonal blocks) rugs: lace each piece to the rug as it is knitted.
- For hexagonal block rugs: lace the rug sections together after all of the pieces have been knitted.
- For "wedge" rugs and the center of round "bullseye" rugs: lace the center hole closed, then lace the edges together.
- For the outer rounds of "bullseye" rugs: lace each section to the rug as it is completed.
- For coil knitted rugs, spool knitted rugs and "idiot cord" rugs: alternate lacing with knitting through the rug construction.

**Step 1: Layout.** Lay the knitted rug sections on the floor in the order they will appear in the rug. You will find that some knitted sections have a better side or appear differently when turned the opposite direction. If you have many sections to lace, pin notes to each piece reminding you of the arrangement.

**Step 2: Strip for Lacing.** Decide which fabric to use for joining. If the pieces contain two contrasting colors of strip, choose the darker or duller color for the joining. Cut a length of strip one-and-one-half times as long as the seam to use for the lacing

**Step 3: Lacing.** Always work on a flat surface. Thread the fabric strip into a lacing, tapestry or weaving needle with a large eye. (Lacking a lacing needle, use a safety pin on the end of the strip for the lacing to use as a needle.) Pin the end of the fabric strip to one end of the knitting leaving about six inches to lace back into the work later.

Insert the lacing needle into the very first loop of the knitting in the corner of one of the knitted sections to be joined. Bring the needle up through the back of the corresponding loop on the other knitted section. Repeat this process to make a snug joint.

Make one whip stitch through both corresponding knitted loops at the ends of the first rows of knitting. Then use one whip stitch to join the second rows of knitting. Continue lacing the ends of corresponding rows until the entire seam is completed. The lacing

## *General Lacing Procedure for Knitted Rugs*

***The easiest way to attach lacing strip securely is to sew it directly to the tail of fabric strip where the knitting stitches were cast on or cast off. Insert the lacing needle threaded with the strip into the matching row on the knitting where the section is to be attached. Pull the strip through. Insert the needle going down into one section and coming up through the other (whip stitch) and repeat matching the knitted rows on each piece.***

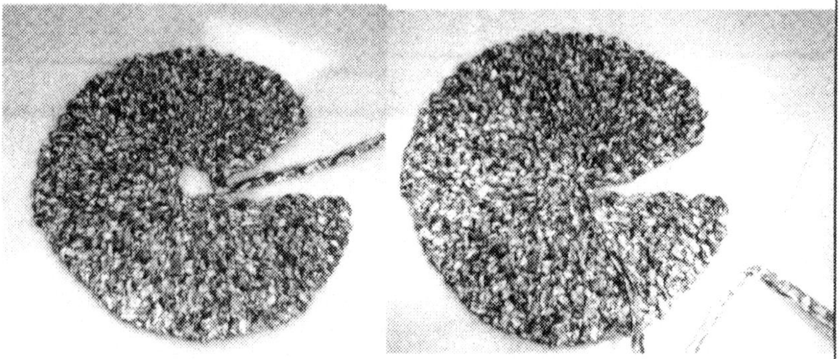

***Round centers for knitted bullseye rugs and the centers of wedge knitted rugs will have a 'hole' in the center when the knitting is completed. Lacing begins at the center passing the lacing needle under the center loops and pulling the hole closed like a drawstring.***

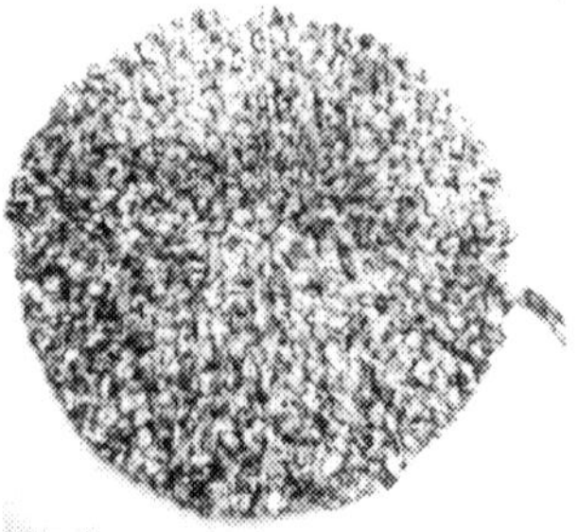

***Then the matching ends of the knitting are laced together using a whip stitch. Shown, above left, is a round center before lacing with the hole open. Above right the center only has been laced to close the hole and at left the matching edges of the round have been laced together to complete the section.***

should be very snug, so that the sections are firmly joined together, but not so tight that the knitting is distorted. Put two whip stitches in the last knitted row, and cut off the fabric strip so about six inches remain.

If you have several pieces to join together, repeat this lacing process until all knitted sections are joined. Then lay the rug on the floor to check that the lacing is not so tight that it keeps the rug from laying flat. Loosen the lacing if necessary.

**Step 4: Finishing.** Lace in all ends of fabric strip. You will have several little "tails" of fabric strip that need to be worked into the rug to finish it—from casting on, casting off and the lacing. Use the same lacing needle as for joining and work these tag ends into the knitting. Sew the ends in place with needle and thread, and clip off any excess very close to the work.

## EDGE FINISHES FOR KNITTED RUGS (WHIP STITCH, BLANKET STITCH, SINGLE CROCHET, SCALLOP, BRAID, FRINGE)

Edging a knitted rug is usually done for decorative purposes. The only exception is a rug knitted with a plain stockinette stitch will have a tendency to curl. Stockinette rugs should have an edging.

If you want to frame your rug, choose a different color for the edging—but use the same type of fabric, prepared in the same way that you did for your rug. All rugs should be completely assembled before you begin edging with all strips or sections already laced together, and the rug blocked if necessary.

A **whip stitch border** is a good choice for a lightweight edging where you simply want to protect the edge of the rug from wear. To edge your rug with a single piece of strip, allow sufficient length to go 2½ times around the rug. For large rugs, that will be too long to handle, so plan on sewing on more strip as needed. Thread the rug strip into a lacing needle. Use a small safety pin to secure the tail end to the rug, leaving about six inches loose. Insert the needle into a knitted stitch at the outside edge and pull the lacing through. Insert the needle into the next stitch and repeat the process. With the whip stitch, the needle is always inserted in the same direction (back to front *or* front to back). At outside corners, insert two stitches. On inside corners, skip a stitch.

## *Edgings for Knitted Rugs*

***For most types of knitted rugs, edgings are optional and are added for decorative purposes. The exception is the plain stockinette stitch which has a tendency to curl and should have an edging. Using a matching fabric strip will make the edging appear to be an integral part of the rug. Contrasting fabrics will show off the edging.***

***The simplest edging is a plain whip stitch worked all of the way around the rug.***

***A blanket stitch edging will protect the rug because it extends outside of the knitted portion. Left handed and right handed stitching above.***

***A single crochet edging is the stiffest and will not only protect the edge of the rug, it will also help a light rug hold its shape.***

When the lacing is complete, insert one more stitch over the very first stitch. Clip off the rug strip so that there is about six inches left. Using the lacing needle, work the ends of the lacing strip back into the knitting and sew them in place with a needle and thread.

A **blanket stitch border** is a good choice for knitted rugs with flat profiles such as woven fabric stitch rugs and corn-on-the-cob rugs. Thread the rug strip into a lacing needle. Use a small safety pin to secure the tail end to the rug, leaving about six inches loose. Insert the needle into a knitted stitch at the outside edge, going in from the front. Move the lacing strip so that it is under and to the left of the point of the needle. Pull the lacing through. There should be a small loop of strip at the top of the stitch, parallel to the rug edge. Insert the needle into the next stitch on the left and repeat the process. (Left handers will find working to the right is easier—keep the loop of strip to the right and move one stitch to the right.) At outside corners, insert two stitches. On inside corners, skip a stitch. When the lacing is complete, insert one more stitch over the very first stitch. Clip off the rug strip so that there is about six inches left. Using the lacing needle work the ends of the lacing strip back into the knitting and sew them in place with a needle and thread.

A **single crochet border** is a good choice for creating a stiff edge on a knitted rug. It also has the advantage of being able to be pulled out and replaced if the edge is heavily worn. The problem with a single crochet border is that crocheting with the fabric will have a different gauge than the knitting, so you have to place your crocheting evenly by eye (not in each knitted stitch). Begin by pinning the end of the edging strip to the rug, leaving about a six-inch tail. Insert the hook into a knitted stitch at the edge, and pull a loop through. Yarn over, and complete the single crochet. Move the hook over and insert it for the next stitch and repeat the single crochet. Keep the crochet stitches as evenly placed as you can. At outside corners, insert three single crochet stitches. On inside corners, skip a stitch. When you have completed crocheting around the rug, slip stitch into the top back thread of the very first crochet stitch. Pull up the strip and end it off by using a lacing needle to work the thread ends back into the work.

Wider borders are made by adding additional rows of single crochet in the same way. Look closely at the strip rug shown in Chapter

3 which includes two rows of a single crochet border, one of each of the same fabrics used in the rug.

A **crocheted scallop border** is fancier way to create a heavy edge but should be used judiciously since the scallops can curl and present a tripping hazard. Rugs with a scalloped edge shouldn't be used in high traffic areas. A scalloped edge is most suitable for round and oval rugs due to the problems of scallop placement at corners. Begin the same way as with a single crochet border.

For each scallop, repeat the sequence: 1 single crochet; 1 double crochet, 1 triple crochet, 1 double crochet. As you approach the last two or three scallops around the edge, check your stitch placement to make sure that you will end with a complete scallop. Slip stitch into the top, back thread of the very first single crochet that you made. Pull the strip up through the stitch and finish off just like the single crochet border.

A **braided border** is probably the most time consuming to make, but is also the showiest. The braid is made separately and then hand sewn to the edge of the knitted rug. If you made the New England Style of the bullseye rug, you'll want to add a braided border so that the rug matches, but braided borders work nicely with just about any type of knitted rug. Any of the flat braids for rugs can be used, but I'll have to refer you to another of my books on rug braids and braiding for the braids of four to twelve strands.

Generally, with a flat profile knitted rug, the braids are made with the 1½-inch prefolded cotton strip. If you are using a knitted fabric in the rug, use the same rug strip as for the rug in the braids.

For higher profile rugs (such as the garter stitch) a thicker braid will appear more in scale with the rug, so cut the strips for the braiding up to twice as wide as used in your knitted rug. Braid the strip sufficiently long to fit around your rug with some extra. Begin sewing the braid to the edge of the rug using a strong hand-sewing thread. (Coats & Clarks, extra strong hand quilting thread is a good choice.) Always begin sewing the braid on a straight side of the rug if it has one. Don't sew the very first three or four inches of the braid. Allow *plenty of ease* in the braid around curves and at corners, or the braided edge will cup. When the braid is sewn almost all of the way around, check the fit of the braid ends.

To match the braid ends together without a lump, the braiding strips will need to be tapered so that they can be interwoven (this is called "butting" the braids). Trim the strip ends to half width for the last four or five inches. Unravel the beginning end of the braid a few turns to do this. Then pin the braid to the rug with safety pins and begin interlacing the braids from both ends. Work carefully and when you are satisfied with the joint, sew the ends in place and carefully clip off any excess. Then sew the joined section to the rug.

A **fringed border** is easy to add to a knitted rug. I will admit though that I am not a fan of fringed borders since they never stay neat. But if you like fringes, here's how to get an even fringe all of the way around. Complete a whip stitch border all of the way around the rug but make the stitches with just a little slack.

Cut fabric strip for the fringes twice as long as you want the fringe to be. Turn the rug over so that the "best" side is down. Fold a fringe strip in half. Insert a crochet hook (size H or J) under a whip stitch, and hook the fold in the fringe. Pull the folded loop under the whip stitch and with that loop on the hook, pull both ends of the fringe through it. Tug lightly on the ends of the fringe to tighten its knot. Fringes can be added to every whip stitch around the outside, but usually it is plenty thick with a fringe added in every other whip stitch. At outside corners, insert the fringes more closely spaced. Usually three fringes are needed right at a corner.

## KNITTING A "FRAME" FOR A RECTANGULAR RUG

A knitted "frame" is an excellent way to finish off a rectangular rug because it eliminates the sharp corners which tend to catch feet and curl up when the rug is in use. A frame can also disguise imperfect matching or lacing of strip or block rugs.

Using a frame of a contrasting color or darket tone will also accent the body of the rug itself. While knitting a frame looks complex, it really isn't. The principles of wedge-knitting form the four corners, with straight knitting along the ends and sides.

Of course, you will want to have your rug completed before you begin to knit the frame. The knitting is done to fit exactly around the completed rug.

*A knitted frame is begun by a short section of garter stitch, which will lay along one side of the finished rug. In this example, the frame is eight stitches wide, so begin with casting on 8 stitches. Use the garter stitch (slip 1, knit 1) and knit the strip to the desired legnth, usually about ten inches from the first corner. The following series of 8 rows are repeated three times to form a right-angle corner in the knitting.*

**Directions to knit a corner (repeat three times):**
Row 1: Knit 2, turn work
Row 2: Slip 1, Knit 1, turn work
Row 3: Knit 4, turn work
Row 4: Slip 1, Knit 3
Row 5: Knit 6, turn work
Row 6: Slip 1, Knit 5
Row 7: Knit 8
Row 8: Slip 1, Knit 7

*When the first corner is completed, resume knitting with the straight garter stitch. Occasionally lay the knitted frame next to the rug to determine when to knit the next corner. When the frame knitting reaches exactly to the next rug corner, it is time to knit three more wedges.*

*Note: the point of the knitting needle should point toward the outside of the frame so that the corner turns the right direction. If the needle points toward the rug itself, knit one more row of garter stitches before beginning the corner sequence.*

*When the second corner is completed, resume regular garter stitches along the third side. Match the knitting to the next corner as above and knit the third corner.*

*Straight garter stitches form the third side, carefully fitting the frame for the fourth corner.*

*Repeat the corner sequence for the fourth corner, and resume straight garter stitches until the frame appears to fit closely around the entire rug.* Do not cast off the knitted stitches. *Instead, use safety pins to secure the frame to the rug and begin lacing the frame and the rug together.*

*As you approach the final section of the frame, check the knitting and add another row or two (or pull out rows) so that the two ends of the frame will match up exactly. Then cast off the knitting. Lace the two ends of the frame together.*

*You can make a larger rug by adding more knitted strips around the frame section. If you are using the garter stitch, subsequent rounds do not need the corners knitted in. Just straight knititng will curve around the rug. See the chapter on Bullseye knitting for adding additional rounds.*

*A frame is knitted separately from the rug, but it must be carefully fitted as it is made.*

## ALTERNATE WAYS TO CAST ON AND CAST OFF

Most knitting is done with the "standard" method of casting on and casting off stitches. Those standard methods are sometimes not suited to rug making. On the following pages are various alternatives to the standard methods and their application is not at all limited to rug making. If you are a beginning knitter particularly, you've probably ended up with too much slack in your first row when you use standard casting on. That problem is eliminated entirely with the use of the single crochet stitch cast on over the needles, so you should give it a try. Also, use the single crochet stitch for casting on when making strip type rugs so that both ends of the strip have the same texture.

If you are planning to add fringes to the ends of strip rugs, use the "just start knitting" method of casting on so that there is enough slack in the initial row to allow for inserting the fringing strip. Of course, the alternate casting off procedure with fringes should be used at the other end.

### *Standard Method of Casting On Stitches*

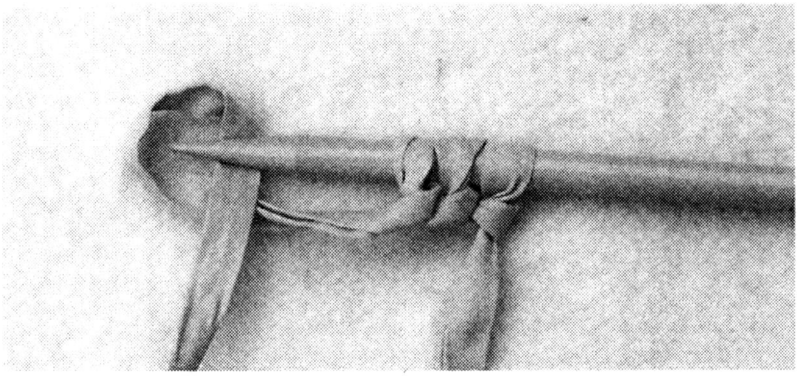

***The standard method of casting on stitches for kniting is to make a slip knot and place it over the needle. Then the strip is twisted into a loop (usually over a finger) and the loop is slipped onto the hook. Standard casting on is fine for ends which will be laced together, such as in the outer bands of bullseye rugs.***

### *Easy Alternate Casting On Using a Chain Stitch*

***Beginning knitters often have difficulty keeping the tension even with the standard method of casting on. The easiest alternative is to crochet a chain with a hook of the same diameter as the needles. Then the knitting needle is slipped through the chain, going through each stitch from front to back. This is an easy way to get a solid end for a strip style rug and will also keep lightweight stitches from curling.***

## *Alternate Casting On: "Just Start Knitting"*

***Of all of the various alternatives for casting on, this is the one that is the most popular with beginners since it is nearly impossible to drop a stitch.***

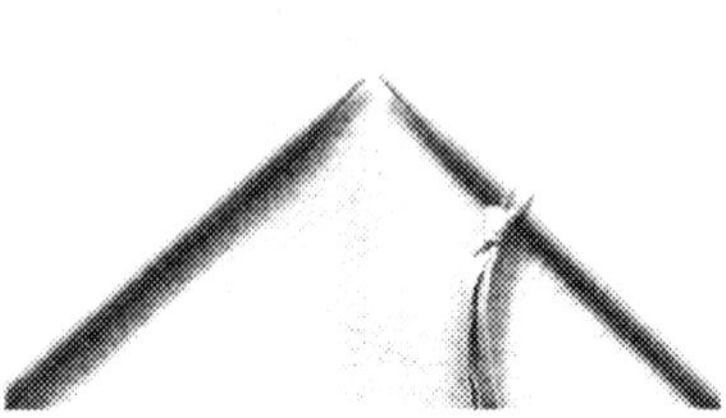

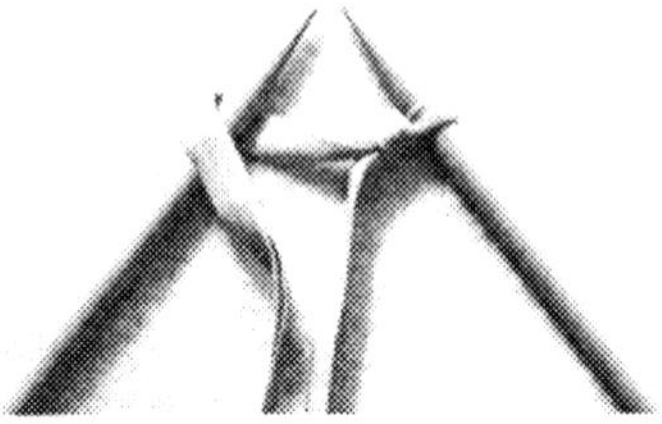

***Begin by making a slip knot on the right needle (left above). Then loop the strip over the left needle (right, above). No twist is needed.***

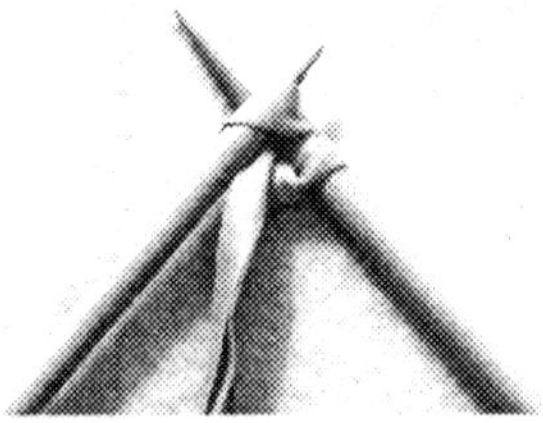

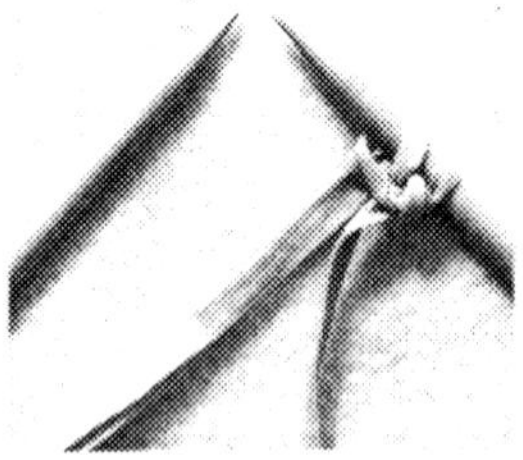

***Insert the righ needle under the strip and the left needle. Notice in the left picture that it is in position to complete a knit stitch. Complete the knit stitch as normal and the stitch passes to the right hand needle as shown above right.***

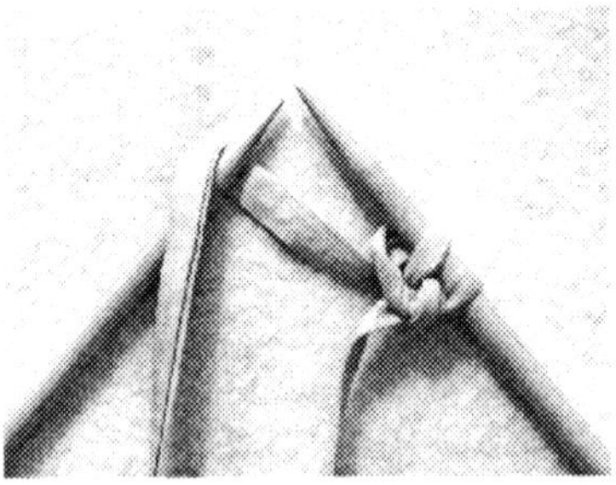

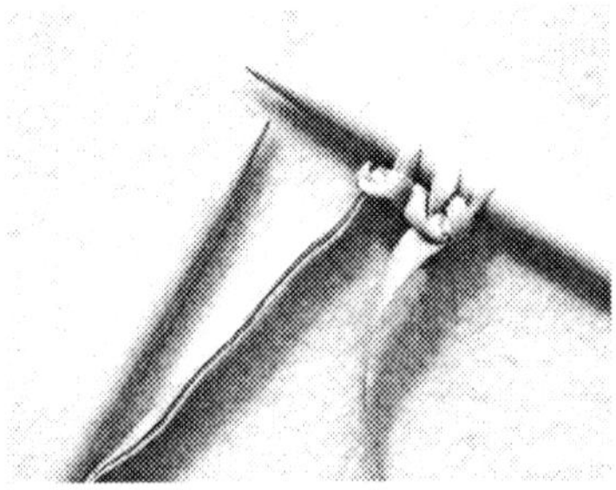

***Repeat the process by bringing the left needle up underneath the strip, inserting the right needle "knitwise" and completing the stitch. Continue until you have the desired number of stitches cast onto the right needle.***

***The only disadvantage to this method of casting on is that it will create slightly looser edge than the standard casting on (done right), so you may want to add an edging to the rug.***

## ***Alternate Casting On with a Single Crochet Stitch***

***Of the various alternate types of casting on procedures for rugs, this one is the best since it has a appearance most like the standard casting off so it will match from end to end in a rug.***

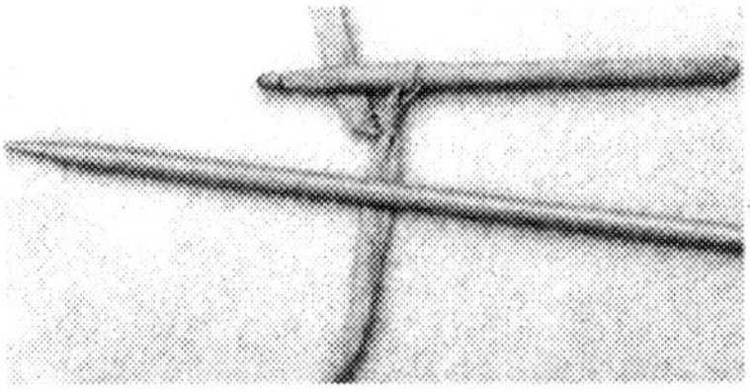

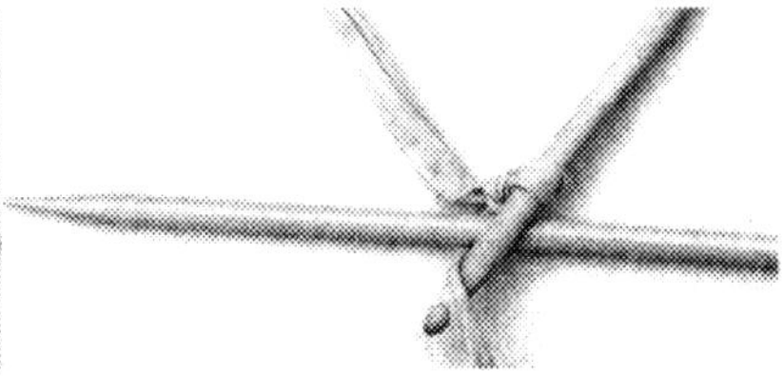

***Begin by making a slip knot over a hook of the same diameter as the knitting needles (left). Pass the strip under the needle and over the hook (right).***

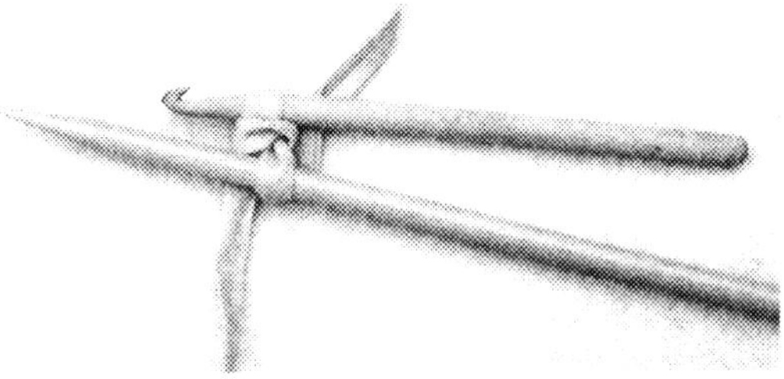

***Pass the strip back under the needle again and pull a loop through both loops on the hook. Shown above is the first single crochet stich completed. Note that the strip is already in the correct position to begin the next single crochet stitch—being underneath the needle on the opposite side from the hook.***

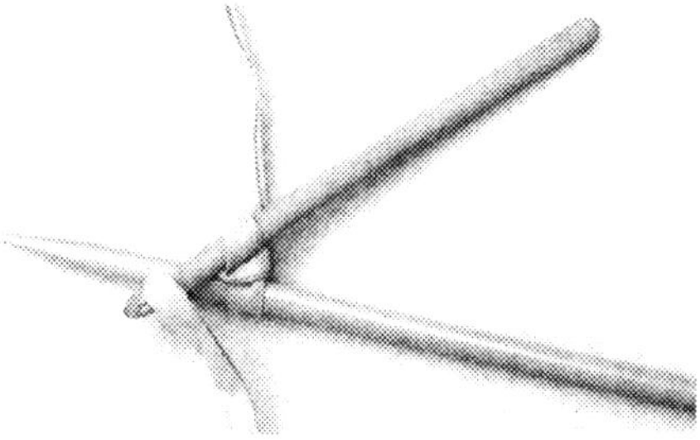

***To make the second stitch, grab the strip with the hook (two loops on the hook) at left. Then bring the strip under the needle, grab the strip again with the hook, and pull that loop through both loops on the hook. Below, several stitches are completed on the needle.***

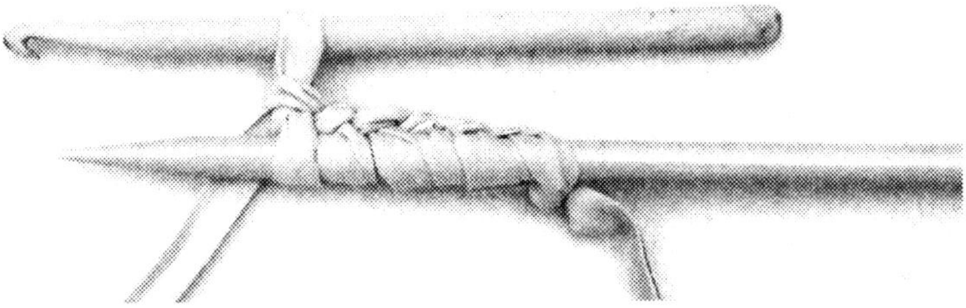

## *Alternate Methods of Casting Off*

***For a flat edge on a thick knitted rug, use the weaving method of casting off.***

***To cast off with weaving, remove the needle from several stitches. Have a lacing needle threaded with matching or contrasting rug strip.***

***Beginning with the first loop, insert the needle up into the loop, then down through the first and second loops.***

***Then bring the needle up through the second and third loops and down through the third and fourth loops.***

***Then up through the fourth and fifth loop and down through the fifth and sixth, and so on, moving over one loop each time.***

***The finished edge is shown with contrasting strip for illustration purposes. This method of casting off really should be done with strip that matches the rug for the neatest effect.***

***Another way to cast off is to insert fringes in each loop that comes off of the needle. The sample shows the process in order from left to right.***

***1. Fold over the fringe piece and pull the fold through a loop.***

***2. Fold the loop over and then bring the ends of the fringe up through it.***

***3. Pull on the ends of the fringe to tighten them.***

# *Afterword*

I suspect that there aren't many authors that ever feel that their book is "done," but there comes a point at which the final period gets placed. I know very well that this book isn't complete because at most it is only a general map of the land of knitted rugs. An entire book could be devoted to any *one* of the techniques covered here—and there probably will be. I hope that I've inspired your own textile explorations with this handbook and your curiosity about the field of rug making.

## Online Resources for Rugmakers:

**For information about rag rugs in general including knitted rugs, the "Rugmakers Homestead" is the best place to start.**
It includes a "Rag Rugs Tour" covering all of the various types of rug making methods. The website also includes articles about rug history, advice on rug making and current links to other resources, suppliers and rug makers. Rug making books, tools and supplies in an online catalog.

**http://www.rugmakershomestead.com**

Halcyon Yarns offer a durable wool yarn especially for making rugs in a large range of colors.

**http://www.halcyonyarn.com**

LACIS offers a wide variety of knitting and other rug making equipment and tools.

**http://www.lacis.com**

# *About the Author*

Trained as a wildlife biologist and with a long family tradition of textile skills, Mrs. Gray has demonstrated a unique talent for researching and being able to reproduce old rug making techniques. Beginning in the 1970s she also experimented with new textile structures and in the 1980s began writing about rug making. When asked about her purpose in documenting the hundreds of rug making methods, she told the *Idaho Art's Journal* in 1987, "I am the door through which others will walk." Her goal has always been to teach others to make rugs and thereby preserve the methods for future generations. Mrs. Gray lives with her husband in the mountains of Idaho.

Printed in the United Kingdom by
Lightning Source UK Ltd., Milton Keynes
138856UK00001B/89/A

9 781931 426251